Christianity: A Very Short Introduction

VERY SHORT INTRODUCTIONS are for anyone wanting a stimulating and accessible way in to a new subject. They are written by experts, and have been published in more than 25 languages worldwide.

The series began in 1995, and now represents a wide variety of topics in history, philosophy, religion, science, and the humanities. Over the next few years it will grow to a library of around 200 volumes – a Very Short Introduction to everything from ancient Egypt and Indian philosophy to conceptual art and cosmology.

Very Short Introductions available now:

ANARCHISM   Colin Ward
ANCIENT EGYPT   Ian Shaw
ANCIENT PHILOSOPHY
   Julia Annas
ANCIENT WARFARE
   Harry Sidebottom
THE ANGLO-SAXON AGE
   John Blair
ANIMAL RIGHTS   David DeGrazia
ARCHAEOLOGY   Paul Bahn
ARCHITECTURE
   Andrew Ballantyne
ARISTOTLE   Jonathan Barnes
ART HISTORY   Dana Arnold
ART THEORY   Cynthia Freeland
THE HISTORY OF
   ASTRONOMY   Michael Hoskin
ATHEISM   Julian Baggini
AUGUSTINE   Henry Chadwick
BARTHES   Jonathan Culler
THE BIBLE   John Riches
BRITISH POLITICS
   Anthony Wright
BUDDHA   Michael Carrithers
BUDDHISM   Damien Keown
CAPITALISM   James Fulcher
THE CELTS   Barry Cunliffe
CHOICE THEORY
   Michael Allingham
CHRISTIAN ART   Beth Williamson
CHRISTIANITY   Linda Woodhead

CLASSICS   Mary Beard and
   John Henderson
CLAUSEWITZ   Michael Howard
THE COLD WAR   Robert McMahon
CONTINENTAL PHILOSOPHY
   Simon Critchley
COSMOLOGY   Peter Coles
CRYPTOGRAPHY
   Fred Piper and Sean Murphy
DADA AND SURREALISM
   David Hopkins
DARWIN   Jonathan Howard
DEMOCRACY   Bernard Crick
DESCARTES   Tom Sorell
DRUGS   Leslie Iversen
THE EARTH   Martin Redfern
EGYPTIAN MYTH   Geraldine Pinch
EIGHTEENTH-CENTURY
   BRITAIN   Paul Langford
THE ELEMENTS   Philip Ball
EMOTION   Dylan Evans
EMPIRE   Stephen Howe
ENGELS   Terrell Carver
ETHICS   Simon Blackburn
THE EUROPEAN UNION
   John Pinder
EVOLUTION
   Brian and Deborah Charlesworth
FASCISM   Kevin Passmore
THE FRENCH REVOLUTION
   William Doyle

STUART BRITAIN John Morrill
TERRORISM Charles Townshend
THEOLOGY David F. Ford
THE TUDORS John Guy

TWENTIETH-CENTURY
  BRITAIN Kenneth O. Morgan
WITTGENSTEIN A. C. Grayling
WORLD MUSIC Philip Bohlman

Available soon:

AFRICAN HISTORY
  John Parker and Richard Rathbone
THE BRAIN Michael O'Shea
BUDDHIST ETHICS
  Damien Keown
CHAOS Leonard Smith
CITIZENSHIP Richard Bellamy
CLASSICAL ARCHITECTURE
  Robert Tavernor
CLONING Arlene Judith Klotzko
CONSCIOUSNESS Sue Blackmore
CONTEMPORARY ART
  Julian Stallabrass
THE CRUSADES
  Christopher Tyerman
DERRIDA Simon Glendinning
DESIGN John Heskett
DINOSAURS David Norman
DREAMING J. Allan Hobson
ECONOMICS Partha Dasgupta
THE END OF THE WORLD
  Bill McGuire
EXISTENTIALISM Thomas Flynn
FEMINISM Margaret Walters
THE FIRST WORLD WAR
  Michael Howard
FOUCAULT Garry Gutting
FUNDAMENTALISM
  Malise Ruthven

HABERMAS Gordon Finlayson
HIROSHIMA
  B. R. Tomlinson
HUMAN EVOLUTION
  Bernard Wood
INTERNATIONAL RELATIONS
  Paul Wilkinson
JAZZ Brian Morton
MANDELA Tom Lodge
THE MIND Martin Davies
MODERN ART David Cottington
NATIONALISM Steven Grosby
PERCEPTION Richard Gregory
PHILOSOPHY OF RELIGION
  Jack Copeland and Diane Proudfoot
PHOTOGRAPHY Steve Edwards
THE RAJ Denis Judd
THE RENAISSANCE Jerry Brotton
RENAISSANCE ART
  Geraldine Johnson
ROMAN EMPIRE
  Christopher Kelly
SARTRE Christina Howells
THE SPANISH CIVIL WAR
  Helen Graham
TIME Leofranc Holford-Strevens
TRAGEDY Adrian Poole
THE TWENTIETH CENTURY
  Martin Conway

For more information visit our web site
www.oup.co.uk/vsi

Linda Woodhead

CHRISTIANITY

A Very Short Introduction

OXFORD
UNIVERSITY PRESS

OXFORD
UNIVERSITY PRESS

Great Clarendon Street, Oxford OX2 6DP

Oxford University Press is a department of the University of Oxford.
It furthers the University's objective of excellence in research, scholarship,
and education by publishing worldwide in

Oxford New York

Auckland Cape Town Dar es Salaam Hong Kong Karachi Kuala Lumpur
Madrid Melbourne Mexico City Nairobi New Delhi Shanghai Taipei Toronto

With offices in

Argentina Austria Brazil Chile Czech Republic France Greece
Guatemala Hungary Italy Japan South Korea Poland Portugal
Singapore Switzerland Thailand Turkey Ukraine Vietnam

Oxford is a registered trade mark of Oxford University Press
in the UK and in certain other countries

Published in the United States
by Oxford University Press Inc., New York

British Library Cataloguing in Publication Data
Data available

Library of Congress Cataloging in Publication Data
Woodhead, Linda.
(Very short introductions)
Christianity : a very short introduction / Linda Woodhead. p. cm.
Incudes bibliographical references and index.
1. Christianity.   I. Title.   II. Series.
BR121.3.W66 2004 230—dc22 2004024149

ISBN-13: 978-0-19-280322-1
ISBN-10: 0-19-280322-0

3 5 7 9 10 8 6 4

Typeset by RefineCatch Ltd, Bungay, Suffolk
Printed in Great Britain by
Ashford Colour Press Ltd, Gosport, Hampshire.

Contents

List of illustrations

Introduction

Christianity has a vast reservoir of resources for shaping life and death. Like most religions it is more capacious and flexible than a philosophical system, and works not only with abstract concepts but with vivid stories, striking images, resonant symbols, and life-shaping rituals. It appeals to heart and senses as well as mind, and offers a range of prompts and provocations for guiding and shaping the lives of individuals and societies. There are nevertheless limits to what can count as Christian, for in opening up some possibilities for life and thought it rules out others.

The first two chapters of this book introduce the basic Christian repertoire. They set out some key themes of Christian life and thought, and indicate the foundational resources with which Christians work. Since Christianity is shaped around a person, Jesus Christ, Chapter 1 outlines the range of ways in which he has been interpreted, and the crucial role these interpretations play in setting the boundaries of Christian thought. The second chapter continues this introductory work, hovering high over Christianity in order to pick out the signs, stories, symbols, and rituals that serve as the basic building blocks of the religion, and offering some preliminary glimpses of their unfolding over 2,000 years of Christian history.

The picture that emerges is of a religion with its origins in an explosion of spiritual energy. This energy – harnessed, focused, and channelled by Jesus Christ – empowered his followers to think, feel, and desire in new ways. In the first centuries of Christian history it gave rise to a wide range of different spiritual groups, ideas, and practices – to many different 'Christianities'. They fall along a spectrum, and this spectrum defines the range of subsequent Christian possibility.

At one end of the spectrum, we have forms of Christianity shaped by reverence for higher power. They focus on a God who infinitely transcends the world and human beings and rules over them. Such Christianity sees the good life – the holy life – as involving sacrifice of one's own (sinful) thoughts, choices, and desires in order to live up to the higher life that God requires. At the other end of the spectrum, we have something different: forms of Christianity that place less emphasis upon God's rule *over* human beings, and more emphasis upon the divine *in* the human. Rather than worship a God who remains high above human life, they focus upon the possibility of the divine coming into being in human life. As such, they place their emphasis not on power from above but power from below; not on power from outside but power from within. Interpretations of Jesus differ accordingly: for a Christianity of higher power, he is a transcendent being who must be obeyed; whereas for a Christianity of inner power, he is a spiritual being who can inspire, in-Spirit, and divinize human life.

Chapters 3 and 4 trace the ways in which these different tendencies within Christianity played out historically down to the dawn of the modern period. Chapter 3 looks at the two most important historical manifestations of a Christianity of higher power: Church Christianity and Biblical Christianity. Chapter 4 considers the development of more inward-looking forms of Christianity, and discusses Mystical Christianity. Together these chapters suggest that an orientation towards higher power became the dominant mode of Christianity from the 4th century onwards, and that it sought to constrain or co-opt more mystical tendencies.

In due course this preference for hierarchical power – in politics as well as religion – would lead to some serious clashes between Christianity and Western modernity. Chapter 5, which tells the story of Christianity in the modern West, considers these confrontations but shows how liberal versions of Christianity proved compatible with an 'enlightened' modernity that ascribed high value to human dignity and the free exercise of human reason. The more serious clash came after the 1960s, when growing emphasis on the authority and importance of the (affective, experiential) inner life of each unique individual proved much harder for Church and Biblical Christianity to digest. As individuals became more inclined to pay attention to inner life and well being, so they became less willing to conform to the 'higher authority' of God, reason, church, or anything else. The result, in most Western countries, has been a gradual decline in Christian belief and a very severe fall in churchgoing in the last quarter of the 20th century.

Outside the West, however, Christianity has experienced much greater success in recent times, as we see in Chapter 6. In much of the southern hemisphere churches have experienced rapid growth since the 1970s, and it is this that has allowed Christianity to retain its status as the world's largest religion, reaching an estimated two billion adherents in 2000. In many parts of the South, 'charismatic' forms of Christianity are flourishing. They combine the clear directives of higher power (the Bible) with the inner empowerment of the Holy Spirit.

The book closes with a chapter that expands on a theme that has been implicit throughout: the roles of women and men in Christianity and the place of the male and the female. It explores the paradox of a religion that has always attracted large numbers of women, but seems to have reserved highest power – on earth and in heaven – for men and the masculine. What we find is that Christianity maintains a fine balance between endorsing male privilege on the one hand, and exalting the female and feminine virtues on the other.

Terms and categories

It is conventional to analyse Christianity in terms of a set of categories generated by the religion itself: 'early Church', 'Protestant', 'Nestorian', 'heretical', and so on. My own study of Christianity over many years, which has involved face-to-face research amongst Christians as well as textual research, has led me to favour a different set of analytical categories (including those of Church, Biblical and Mystical Christianity). Since this is an introductory book, I have tried to strike a balance between introducing my own terms and categories and employing more conventional ones. The intention is to offer the reader a fresh perspective on Christianity, whilst indicating how this relates to approaches with which he or she may already be familiar and which may be encountered elsewhere.

Warts and all

There is a tendency in some treatments of Christianity to look only at the positive: the religion's growth, achievements, beliefs, rituals, great men, cultural contributions. Such topics are often treated in isolation from their wider social and material contexts. This book takes a less idealistic approach. It acknowledges that Christianity, like all religions, has to do with ('sacred') power, and it looks at the ways in which such power has been understood, embodied, and exercised – as well as how it has interacted with secular power.

Power in itself is neither good nor bad, merely the force that gets things done. What is interesting, and a focus of the pages that follow, is the range of ways in which it may be understood and activated: as a dominating force that compels its objects, for example, or as a love that 'moves' and is 'moved' in a very different fashion. Since different forms of Christianity have aligned themselves around these different tendencies, this volume considers the full internal diversity of Christianity, and the frequently antagonistic relations between its different strands. It also pays attention to the decline as well as the growth of Christianity, discussing not only its rise to become the world's largest religion, but the serious difficulties it currently faces in the West. The intention throughout is not to pass judgement, but to present a realistic portrait.

Chapter 1
Jesus: the God-man

At first sight the figure of Jesus Christ might seem to serve as a focus of unity for the Christian faith. Whatever else they might disagree about, Christians are at least united in believing that Jesus has a unique significance. Look more closely, however, and it becomes apparent that this focus of unity can also be a cause of division. Though Christians agree that Jesus is significant, they may interpret his significance differently. Despite the strenuous attempts that have continually been made to contain him within a single interpretative framework, he always threatens to break free.

Some of this elusiveness may be traced back to Jesus himself. When he talked he often spoke in riddles and parables, and when asked who he was, he replied: 'who do you say I am?'. He laid down few clear rules, left no systematic body of teaching, and founded no school to pass on his wisdom. The mystery is also a function of the sources on which we have to rely. We cannot consult the books Jesus wrote because he wrote no books, and we cannot turn to contemporary accounts of his life and works for there are no such accounts. We have only interpretations, and interpretations of interpretations. Our most important sources of information are already embroiled in the debate about his significance, and already take sides. What is more, where Jesus is concerned the parameters of interpretation are particularly broad. It is hard enough to give a reliable account of the life of any individual; biographers make a living out of the fact that there can never be a single, definitive interpretation. But when considering Jesus, the difficulty is multiplied, for the issue is not simply 'what sort of a man are we dealing with?' but 'are we dealing with man or God?'. This chapter will review the answers that were given to this question in the first centuries after Jesus' death, answers that would prove enormously influential for subsequent Christian thought and life.

The gospel truth

The earliest and most important sources of written information about Jesus are gospels. The genre is peculiar to early Christianity, and its name gives a clue to its intention, for 'gospel' translates the Greek word *euangelion* meaning 'good news'. This word was rarely used in pre-Christian times, except in Roman political propaganda, usually with reference to an emperor. To the extent that they aim to propagate a particular, exalted view of the person they describe, Christian gospels are also propaganda. They tell their readers (or hearers) that Jesus was something special, and they expect them to respond accordingly. No neutral stance is possible in relation to a gospel. Depending on your response, its message will turn out either to be good news for you – or bad.

There were many gospels and many different accounts of Jesus – just as there were many types of early Christian community that produced them. Today only a few of these gospels survive. The most familiar are those of Matthew, Mark, Luke, and John because by the 4th century they had been gathered together, deemed authoritative ('canonical') and included in the 'New Testament'. The latter (written in Greek) was bound together with the 'Old Testament' (the scriptures of the Jewish people written in Hebrew but appropriated by Christianity in an expanded Greek version) to form the Christian Bible. This was just one step in the long historical process whereby one version of Christianity came to establish itself as the authoritative, 'catholic' (universal) form of 'church', and to win out over its rivals. Once this happened, it was possible to draw a

1. Gospels were first circulated as 'codexes', small books made from papyrus. Many early Christian communities probably possessed only a single codex, perhaps a gospel or a 'harmony' of several gospels. It would be many centuries before churches possessed a complete New Testament or Bible. This early fragment from Matthew's Gospel probably dates from early in the 3rd century CE.

distinction between canonical gospels and 'apocryphal' ones, and to downgrade the importance of the latter. But in the earliest centuries after Jesus' death it was possible for any Christian group to produce its own gospel, thereby securing its particular understanding of Jesus and the life he inspired. A few of these apocryphal gospels have survived, including the very early Gospel of Thomas, which is considered briefly in this chapter. They serve to remind us that the Jesus depicted in the New Testament gospels was not the only Jesus who was remembered and revered in early Christian circles.

Possible dating of the earliest written sources on which our knowledge of Jesus depends

(birth of Jesus c. 4 BCE, death of Jesus c. 30 CE)

30–60 CE
Paul's letters (Epistles)
A sayings source, 'Q', now lost, but used by Luke and Matthew
A miracles source now lost, but used by Mark and John
Earliest layer of the Gospel of Thomas

60–80 CE
The Gospel of Mark
Additional material in the Gospel of Thomas

80–120 CE
The Gospel of Matthew (c. 90)
The Gospel of Luke (c. 90)
The Gospel of John (c. 100–110)

120–150 CE
The Book of Acts
Other New Testament Epistles including the Pastoral Epistles and Catholic Epistles

The authorized version

For now, however, let us confine our attention to the authorized version of Christian truth, the version that was propagated by the winning side, became canonical, and has informed the views of a majority of Christian believers ever since. It is here that we find the most influential answers to the question of who Jesus really was, and here that we encounter the Jesus who has inspired more lives and worked more miracles than the elusive 'historical Jesus' who historians struggle endlessly to recreate.

The canonical gospels combine stories about Jesus with records of his teaching. Despite important variations between them, they share a common narrative thread and a common purpose. The narrative falls roughly into two halves. The first establishes Jesus as a teacher and miracle worker in Galilee (the northern province of Israel). Though baptized by John the Baptist, he launches an independent career and wins his own followers. Jesus works amongst his people, the Jews, and acknowledges their God and scriptures. He offers an interpretation of the Jewish faith that is critical towards the religious elite but favourable to those who are destitute, humble, of no account. The second part of the narrative shifts to Jerusalem in Judea (the southern part of Israel), where Jesus' provocative ministry alarms the governing authorities (the Romans, supported by Jewish leaders) and leads to his arrest, trial, and execution. He is crucified as a criminal and buried in a tomb. When some of his followers visit the grave three days later, they find it empty. Miraculous appearances by Jesus convince his followers that God has raised him from the dead. The Book of Acts (written by the author of Luke's gospel) continues the story in the New Testament, recounting how Jesus, having ascended into heaven, pours out his Spirit on his followers at Pentecost and brings into being the Christian community.

The common narrative thread reflects the gospels' common purpose: to persuade that Jesus was no mere mortal, that he was uniquely favoured by God, that he has transcended the limitations of normal human life, and that those who dedicate their lives to him may share in the eternal life he now enjoys. To press the message home the gospels marshal the most convincing evidence they can find. It falls into four main categories: teaching, miracles, resurrection, and fulfilled prophecy.

Teaching

Jesus' teaching testifies to his immersion in the religion and culture of the Jewish people. The followers of an exclusivistic monotheism, their identity was based on the belief that God (Yahweh) had called them out of all the nations, made them His chosen people, granted them the land of Israel for their exclusive possession, and given them the Law (Torah) by which to live. Successive foreign occupations of Israel were often interpreted as punishment for failure to observe the Law. In Jesus' day, with Israel under Roman occupation, a wide range of Jewish teachers, groups, and movements attempted to make sense of this latest episode in the stormy history of God's chosen people.

Jesus taught that far from abandoning His people, God's reign (*basileia*, usually translated 'kingdom') was imminent. Speaking almost exclusively to fellow Jews, he told them to be watchful of the signs of the times and to ready themselves for the new Godly society that was being prepared. Readiness consists in living as if God's will and law were already in force – by observing the spirit rather than the letter of the law, its essence rather than its every detail. And the essence of God's law, according to Jesus, is love without limits. God is calling His people to love as he loves: perfectly and without limitation. Those who do so join the family of God, whose ties and loyalties surpass those of any natural form of human association, including the biological family.

Although addressed to the individual and calling for a personal change of heart, Jesus' message envisages a universal society bound together by divine love. Replacing limited human ties of affection based on kinship, ethnic identity, and self-interest with the unlimited love of God, it is an egalitarian kingdom of love without limits. Jesus likens it to a family in which all are brothers and sisters of one another and children of the one Father ('Abba', Jesus' preferred name for God). When God's reign begins on earth it will be those who are sufficiently humble to accept their need for divine love and forgiveness who will find that they belong to this order of things, whereas the proud, self-righteous, and unjust will be exposed as citizens of an alternative order. Thus the first will be last, and the last will be first.

Extracts from Jesus' teaching: Matthew 5 and Luke 14

You have heard that it was said, 'You shall love your neighbour and hate your enemy.' But I say to you, Love your enemies and pray for those who persecute you, so that you may be sons of your Father who is in heaven; for He makes His sun rise on the evil and the good, and sends his rain on the just and on the unjust.

If anyone comes to me and does not hate his own father and mother and wife and children and brothers and sisters, yes, even his own life, he cannot be my disciple.

Miracles

Since Jesus' teaching points away from his person towards the kingdom of love that he proclaims, it leaves the question of his status open. The gospels record a few sayings in which Jesus makes explicit reference to his own unique significance (though there is extensive debate amongst scholars about their authenticity). Some of these sayings suggest that Jesus is ordained by God to inaugurate the divine rule on earth. Others have Jesus openly declare that he is the 'Son of God'. John's gospel goes furthest by including long discourses in which Jesus reflects on his divine status (the 'I am . . .' discourses). In other gospel passages it is other people who announce Jesus' unique status – as Peter does when Jesus is transfigured, and the centurion when he witnesses Jesus' death.

More important than words in establishing Jesus' extraordinary status are miracles. The gospel narratives are full of accounts of Jesus' miraculous deeds. They linger lovingly over the detail, and they lay great emphasis on the way in which witnesses react with awe and wonder. Some of the miracles involve human healing, while others demonstrate Jesus' control over natural events – stilling the storm, walking on water, feeding five thousand. Since the Jewish people believed that God alone had ultimate control over the world, the clear implication was that God was at work in Jesus. Even those who are not convinced by Jesus' miracles admit that some supernatural power must be at work – if not God, then Beelzebub the devil.

Resurrection

The greatest miracle of all is the resurrection, and it is no surprise that three of the four gospels make it their climax (Mark's gospel was quickly amended to ensure that it too ended with stories of the risen Christ). Just as Jews believed that only God could work real miracles, so they believed that only God could raise a human being from the dead. There was also widespread belief that God would only do this at the end of time; the first resurrection would inaugurate a more general resurrection as history was brought to its close. Thus Jesus' resurrection would signal to those who believed in it that God's power was at work in this man in a special way. It would confirm that Jesus had a unique role in the divine plan for the world, and that through his work the long reign of suffering and oppression was about to come to an end.

Fulfilled prophecy

Jesus' resurrection gained its meaning by being interpreted in the context of Jewish prophecy and expectation. Since the same was true for the other events of his life and death, the gospel writers are at pains to show that all these things happened in accordance with the Jewish scriptures. If, as the Jewish people believed, God was in control of history, and the prophets had some insight into the direction in which He was leading it, then they must have foretold the life, death, and resurrection of Jesus Christ. So intense is the gospels' concern to demonstrate this logic that some of the stories about Jesus actually seem to have been shaped or even generated by a prophecy. This is particularly clear in the stories that the gospels of Luke and Matthew supply about Jesus' appearance on earth – including the conception by a virgin (Mary), the birth in a stable in Bethlehem, the visit of wise men, and the flight into Egypt.

It was not only Jews who might be convinced by being shown how 'these things took place to fulfil what the prophets foretold'. The Jewish faith and scriptures were also held in high regard by some Romans, who admired their morality and antiquity. By presenting itself as the fulfilment of Jewish hope, Christianity might win a more favourable hearing than if it were perceived to be a novelty – what we might call a 'new religious movement'. To show that Jesus' life, death, and resurrection took place in accordance with prophecy, would thus be to transfer some of the weighty authority of the ancient Jewish scriptures to him and the community that gathered around his memory.

Who do you say I am?

The earliest gospel, Mark, portrays the most human Jesus, and the latest, John, the most thoroughly divine. But all the New Testament gospels agree that Jesus stood in such a uniquely close relationship to God that he alone crosses the line that separates creatures from the God who made them. This emphasis on Jesus' divinity is echoed and reinforced in the other documents of the New Testament, including the epistles of Paul. The latter, written by an aspiring early Christian leader to various groups of Christians around the Mediterranean, barely refer to the earthly Jesus. Their focus is the risen Jesus, the 'Lord' who dwells in the heavens and is present on earth in the Spirit. Similarly, the Book of Revelation that ends the New Testament portrays Jesus as the heavenly Lamb who stands by the throne of God and returns to judge the earth at the end of time, precipitating terrible destruction before the heavenly Jerusalem finally descends to earth and God's triumphal reign begins.

To read the New Testament as a whole is thus to be left in no doubt that those who compiled it and deemed it scriptural were the champions of a version of Christianity that wished to stress the divinity of Christ and the almighty power of the God on whose right hand the Son now sits. But there were other options open to those who came into contact with Jesus. As they were expressed in the earliest Christian centuries, they fall into four main categories – which have shaped interpretation of the elusive figure of Jesus ever since.

1. A 'mere' human being

Although Jesus taught and ministered amongst the Jewish people in Palestine, there were many – the majority – who refused to accept that he was anything more than a man. There were many itinerant teachers and miracle workers operating in the same area at the same time, many of whom proclaimed the coming rule of God. Some were crucified by the Romans as well. What made Jesus so special?

'Gentile' (non-Jewish) inhabitants of the Roman Empire might be equally sceptical. If even Jesus' own countrymen regarded the claims made on his behalf as ridiculous, who were they to disagree? Palestine was a small but troublesome region in the Empire, and Jewish radicals were continually inciting their people to rebel against the Romans (such rebellion gave rise to the Jewish wars of 66–70 CE and 132–5 CE). Like Jesus, some of these radicals came from the lowest strata of society, and some preached a primitive communism. Romans of the ruling classes were bound to be suspicious. What mattered to them was this world not the next; the

Empire not the Kingdom. Those whose views have been recorded – the more educated and philosophical – found the Christian appeal to miracles and resurrection manipulative, the sighing after another world misguided, the worship of a God-man demeaning, and the emphasis on faith irrational.

As a footnote, it is worth recording that the tendency of modern historical scholarship has been to reinforce such scepticism about the New Testament's more exalted claims for Jesus. As information about the Mediterranean world in the 1st century CE has increased, scholars have pointed out numerous parallels with Jesus' life and teaching, and have attempted to show that no supernatural causes need be invoked to explain the nature of his career, the expectations that gathered around him, or his execution at the hands of the Romans. They have turned the argument from prophecy on its head by claiming that the gospels' birth and resurrection narratives can be explained as attempts to fit Jesus' life into the logic of Jewish expectation. And they have offered sociological explanations of how and why Jesus' followers turned him into a supernatural being at the centre of a cult. Like many others in the first centuries of the Christian era, they may be prepared to accept that Jesus was a remarkable and inspiring human being, but most (not all) are reluctant to go further – on existing evidence at least.

2. A human being exalted by God

There were other close contemporaries of Jesus who were prepared to accept that he was something special, even though they would not go so far as to proclaim him divine.

The idea that God might bless and exalt a man (rarely a woman) was a commonplace of Jewish thought. The scriptures contained many such examples: Abraham, Moses, and, above all, the righteous ruler of ancient Israel, King David. So central was the figure of the chosen and favoured king in Jewish history that many prophecies had come to focus on the figure of a coming 'messiah' who would deliver Israel from all its troubles and oppression.

Though there were many different conceptions of what the messiah would be like, he was generally viewed in largely human terms as a mighty man anointed by God to fulfil the divine purpose on earth.

Given the heightened climate of messianic expectation in Jesus' day, it was relatively easy for some of his earliest Jewish followers to view him as the long-awaited messiah approved by God. The Greek word 'Christ', which translates the Hebrew word 'Messiah', is one of the first titles associated with Jesus, possibly during his own lifetime. We know that there were many early Christian groups who remained faithful to the Jewish Law and its ritual observances, and who continued to consider themselves Jews. What set these 'Jewish Christians' apart from their fellows was their belief that the messiah had appeared in Jesus of Nazareth and would shortly return to inaugurate God's Kingdom. We know from the New Testament that Paul came into conflict with such Christians when he took the gospel to Gentiles and relaxed the demands of the Jewish law, including circumcision. Though Paul's strategy eventually won the day, there is evidence that groups of Jewish Christians continued to exist for many centuries to come. Their interpretation of Jesus as a man exalted by God also found expression in the early Christian doctrine of 'adoptionism' – the belief that Jesus Christ was a righteous human being who had been adopted and anointed by God.

3. A divine being come to help others become divine

The reason many Jews could accept that Jesus was special but not that he was divine was that the Jewish faith is strictly monotheistic. Though a human being can be called by God, exalted by God, adopted by God, resurrected and caught up into the heavens, he will still be a human – for there is and only ever can be one God.

In Hellenistic culture, however, the boundaries between divine and human were less clearly set. This was the dominant culture of the Roman Empire in Jesus' day, and it drew its inspiration from the cultural legacy of the Ancient Greeks ('Hellenes'). (Much Jewish culture was also influenced by Greek thought, and the division

between Jewish and Hellenistic should not be too sharply drawn.)
Hellenistic culture knew many deities, not just one, and its
gods and goddesses presented themselves as larger-than-life
characters in whom human virtues and vices were magnified.
Since the deities often took human form and mingled with
mortals, and there was regular traffic between heaven and earth,
it was easy enough to fit Jesus into this frame of reference – if
one was persuaded there were grounds for thinking of him as
more-than-human. And since there were so many divine beings,
one could accept that Jesus was divine without necessarily believing
that he was unique.

We know that there were many different groups in the first
centuries of the Christian era who were inspired by what they heard
about Jesus and happy to admit that he had brought the sacred
into the midst of life. Though they were later classified by the
'orthodox' form of Christianity that produced the New Testament
as 'heretical' and 'gnostic', they were more diverse in belief and
organization than these blanket terms suggest – as we will see in
Chapter 4. What many shared was the view that Jesus imparted a
special wisdom ('gnosis') that could help human beings unlock the
sacred potential of their own lives. Rather than viewing him as a
God who must be worshipped, they therefore viewed him as a
divine being who could help individuals get in touch with 'the god
within' – the divine potential that lies at the heart of the human.

Gnostic groups existed alongside other forms of early Christianity
for several centuries. They wrote gospels (like the Gospel of
Thomas), formed canons of scripture, and some developed
sophisticated theology that drew on Greek philosophical
themes. Where they differed from orthodox Christianity and its
interpretation of Jesus was in their view that human beings were
potentially divine. This message had radical, disruptive, and
egalitarian possibilities. Later writers attacked the gnostics for the
way in which they treated women as equals, became arrogant with
their own knowledge, and threatened to undermine established

forms of authority. Recently discovered gnostic scriptures, most notably from Nag Hammadi in Upper Egypt, reveal that gnosticism drew on female as well as male imagery in speaking of the divine, that it often questioned established ways of thinking about human and divine hierarchies, and that it presented Jesus as a teacher who sought not to humble but to exalt his followers. In all these respects it challenged the versions of Christianity that found expression in the New Testament and the church that supported it.

Extract from the Gospel of Thomas (Saying 3)

Jesus says, 'If your leaders say to you, "Look, the Father's rule is in the sky," then the birds of the sky will precede you. If they say to you, "It is in the sea," then the fish will precede you. Rather the Father's rule is inside you and outside you. When you know yourselves, then you will be known, and you will understand that you are children of the living Father. But if you do not know yourselves, you live in poverty, and you are the poverty.'

---

4. The unique God-man

None of the above views represent the New Testament's interpretation of Jesus' significance. This finds its earliest and in many ways its most systematic expression in Paul's letters. Paul's view differs from both adoptionism and gnosticism, and it helped mark the boundaries of what, after the extended period of struggle that will be reviewed in the following chapters, would eventually be established as orthodox 'Christology' (literally, 'words/thought about Christ').

Paul was a Jew, and he accepts the monotheism of the Jewish scriptures. He believes that there is only one almighty, male, creator God and that all creatures are subordinate to him – as a pot is to a potter. If God is displeased with what he has made, he can smash it and begin his work again. This rules out the gnostic route for Paul, for it would be impossible for him to affirm that humans contain the inherent potential to be reunited with their divine source. But Paul is also unable to rest content with an adoptionist Christology, for he believes that Jesus has a connection with God that is closer and more intrinsic.

For Paul, Jesus is connected to God in a way in which no other human being ever has been, can be, or will be. He is not in the heavens with God because God chose to dignify his humanity – he was with God from the beginning of time and all things were created in and through him. He is, in other words, nothing less than the ordering principle of the universe, the timeless divine wisdom by and through which all things were made, and the image of that perfect divine humanity that is the goal and purpose of the whole creation. He is God even more than he is man.

Unlike gnostic inner Christianity, the Pauline view presents human beings not with the challenge of realizing their own divinity by going within, but with the duty of looking upward toward 'the Lord' (Paul's preferred title for Jesus and for God) who alone can save them from their destiny of sin and death. Such salvation can only come about if creatures are prepared to renounce their own judgement, will, and desire in order to be possessed by the Spirit of Christ (the 'Holy Spirit'). For although human beings have no natural ability to become a 'Son of God' like Christ, by supernatural grace they may be transformed into new beings – 'sons by adoption' in Paul's terms. Humans are saved not by their own power or potential, but by being ruled by Christ and living in, through, and for him rather than for themselves. For Paul, the ritual of water baptism symbolizes the death of the old self and the birth of a new Christ-like self. After baptism, as Paul puts it, 'it is no longer I who live, but Christ who lives in me'. The baptized do not become gods in their own right, but members of 'the body of Christ' – parts of a divine collectivity under the headship of Christ. Their

2. Mosaic of Christ from St Peter's Basilica, Vatican City (3rd century CE). Early Christian art borrowed images from classical mythology in order to depict Jesus as a divine being. Here he appears as Apollo/the sun god.

transformation begins on earth, but will culminate in their resurrection from the dead.

For Paul, then, Jesus is the unique God-man – with the emphasis on 'God'. Though truly human, he is divine in a way no other human being ever can be. His humanity, though affirmed, tends to be subsumed and subordinated to his divinity, as it is in the equally 'high' Christology of John's Gospel. The distinction between God and humanity is preserved, as is the necessity of human subordination. Humans are saved not by their own powers, but by the power of the God to whom they must submit, the work of Christ which they must accept with faith, and the power of the Spirit which must take control of their lives.

Extract from Paul's Letter to the Galatians

When we were children, we were slaves to the elemental spirits of the universe. But when the time had fully come, God sent forth His Son, born of a woman, born under the Law, to redeem those who were under the Law, so that we might receive adoption as Sons. And because you are sons, God has sent the Spirit of His Son into our hearts, crying, 'Abba! Father!'.

Extract from John's Gospel

And the Word became flesh and dwelt among us, full of grace and truth; we have beheld His glory, glory as of the only Son from the Father . . . No one has ever seen God; the only Son, who is in the bosom of the Father, He has made Him known.

Conclusion

The spiritual energy harnessed and unleashed by the life, ministry, teaching, and memory of Jesus gave rise to a range of interpretations of his significance, and with them a range of different 'Christianities'. Amongst the latter there were those which saw in Jesus a stimulus to realize one's own divine nature and unite with one's spiritual source. For them, the God-man was a dazzling provocation to seek the divine within. There were others which held that the God-man should be worshipped not emulated, and which placed more stress on his unique divinity than his common humanity. For them, the God-man reinforced belief that God was above rather than within, and that He must be obeyed and revered. And in between these poles were those which agreed that salvation must come from above and must cleanse and destroy our sinful human nature, but nevertheless believed that the divine – as Holy Spirit – could enter within the human to render it more Christ-like.

All these interpretations would be carried forward into Christianity and shape its course in the coming centuries. The first view – the inner, mystical, more gnostic version of Christianity – lay at the margins of what came to be considered orthodox, whilst the 'higher' Christology was gradually identified with the orthodox cause. But at some point in time each and every one of the positions along the spectrum would find its champions and win its supporters. And the interactions between them, and between them and wider society, would shape the course of Christian history.

Chapter 2

The signs and symbols
of Christianity

The previous chapter introduced Christianity by sketching the range of ways in which Jesus was first understood and interpreted. This chapter continues the introductory task by offering a brief overview of how the Christian ritual and symbolic universe developed on the basis of these foundations – in particular, how it developed around the orthodox vision of the unique God-man.

What is presented here is very much an 'ideal type' – a generalization arrived at by singling out features common to the most influential types of Christianity and ignoring their variations. Although the signs, symbols, stories, and rituals described are those most widely shared amongst the different branches of Christianity they are made manifest in different ways. Christianity in the East, for example, places less emphasis on sin than the Western churches, whilst Biblical churches often give relatively little space to sacraments and liturgy and formal ritual in general, and some forms of Mystical Christianity do away with these 'externals' of religion altogether. In this chapter such differences will be downplayed; they are the focus of the chapters that follow.

Sin

According to the New Testament, the 'good news' is that a unique God-man has come to earth, revealed himself to the world, and offered to save all those who dedicate their lives to him. This only counts as good news, however, if you also believe in some very bad news: that human beings need to be saved from something, and are incapable of saving themselves. The more you emphasize the unique and indispensable role of the God-man, the church that bears his name, and those who speak on his behalf, the more you need there to be a problem so serious that only they can put it right.

The New Testament already had a name for the problem – 'sin' – but it was the theologian and bishop Augustine of Hippo (354–430 CE) who breathed life into the concept by placing it within the framework of a story of immense power: the story of the 'Fall'. Augustine's account had its basis in the Old Testament, in the narrative of Genesis 3 which recounts how the first human beings, Adam and Eve, were brought into being by God in an earthly paradise, the Garden of Eden. Though they live in the closest communion with God, He forbids them to eat from the tree at the centre of the garden: the tree of the knowledge of good and evil. But Eve, tempted by the serpent, eats and encourages Adam to do likewise. As a result, Genesis tells us, God removes them from the garden:

> 'Behold, the man has become like one of us, knowing good and evil; and now, lest he put forth his hand and take also of the tree of life, and live for ever' – therefore the Lord God sent him forth . . .

Life east of Eden is very different from life in paradise. Adam must toil and sweat to cultivate a soil that bears thorns and thistles; Eve is condemned to bring forth children in pain; and both are destined to return to the dust from whence they came.

It was – and is – possible to interpret this story in a variety of ways. Therein lies much of its power. One obvious reading is that the story speaks of the infancy of the human race, and that the eating of the fruit represents not only loss of innocence but entrance

3. *Eve, the Serpent and Death* by Hans Baldung Grien (c.1520–5). In this late medieval depiction, Eve enters willingly into a pact with the serpent (the devil) and with death; not only is she tempted, she is also temptress.

into adulthood – with the burdens that brings. Augustine interpreted the story very differently. For him it was bad news through and through. Adam and Eve should have remained in the garden forever, living in unquestioning obedience to the God who knew what was best for them. Their action is utterly sinful; not an admirable grasping at knowledge but a damnable disobedience. What is worse, and here Augustine moves well beyond what the original narrative supplies, their action has corrupted their very nature, and this corruption has been inherited by every member of the human race. (Augustine believed not only that Adam and Eve were the real, biological parents of the human race, but that their sin was transmitted by way of sexual reproduction.)

Bad news indeed. If Augustine was right – and orthodoxy in the West was quick to insist that he was – then every human being is received into the world as damaged goods. So serious is the damage that there is nothing they can do to put it right. All they can do is repent of their own deepest instincts and desires – above all sexual desire – and throw themselves on the mercy of their saviour, Jesus Christ, and the church that mediates his saving grace.

Not all Christians were prepared to go all the way with Augustine. As we will see in Chapter 4, Eastern Christianity did not accept Augustine's belief in the total corruption of human beings. In the West, too, there were some theologians, including Thomas Aquinas, who argued that 'post-lapsarian' (after the Fall) human beings still retained the ability to discern the existence of God and distinguish basic right from wrong (see Chapter 3). Nevertheless, Christianity across the ages tended to accept the main thrust of an Augustinian interpretation by endorsing the view that humans are ultimately powerless to save themselves. If we are not to live wretched lives on earth, and still more wretched lives in the hell that awaits us after death, we require the assistance of a heavenly saviour.

4. *The Way of Good and Evil*, American woodcut (1826). This allegory depicts the few who pass through the cross of Christ to heaven, and the many who walk into the fires of hell.

Even as late as the 19th century, Christians were still producing paintings, sermons, tracts, fiction, and hymns that depicted the 'bad news' in the most vivid fashion. Some gave expression to the total depravity and unutterable wickedness of 'the heart of man', whilst others depicted the torments that awaited the unrepentant sinner in lurid terms. Even though depictions of hell have become less common in Christian circles today, the belief in human sinfulness remains. Most liturgies (the written scripts of worship services) still begin with a confession of sinfulness, and many hymns continue to reinforce the message.

The saviour

The worse the bad news, the better and more welcome the good news. The deeper the sin of Adam, the higher the triumph of Christ. 'O felix culpa . . . ' exclaims the Latin Mass of the Roman Catholic Church, 'oh happy sin which has received as its reward so great and so good a redeemer'. For a Christianity of higher power, the saviour was quickly exalted high above the human condition – and has remained there ever since. Despite clear doctrinal insistence that he is 'very God and very man' (see Chapter 3), his divinity has tended to eclipse and qualify his humanity rather than vice versa.

This early stress on Christ's divine status may explain why there are no records of what the human Jesus looked like. It certainly explains why the earliest visual representations of Christ, from the 2nd century, present him as a god rather than a man, and borrow directly from Graeco-Roman art (as in Figure 2 in the previous chapter). When Christianity finally began to develop its own images of Jesus, from the 4th century onwards, the figure of a slim, pale, bearded, robed, long-haired, ethereal man emerged, and has remained definitive to this day. Though this Jesus has a human face, it is no ordinary face. His expression is impassive, his gaze disconcertingly direct,

Christian confessions of sin

We have followed too much the devices and desires
    of our own hearts,
We have offended against thy holy laws,
We have left undone those things which we ought to
    have done,
And we have done those things which we ought not to
    have done,
And there is no health in us.

> General confession from the *Book of
> Common Prayer* (Anglican)

Repent, and live: despair and trust!
Jesus for you to death was sold;
Though hell protest, and earth repine,
He died for crimes like yours – and mine.

> Verse of a Methodist hymn (by Charles Wesley)

Original sin is the corruption of nature of every man,
that naturally is engendered of the offspring of Adam,
whereby man is very far gone from original righteous-
ness, and of his own nature inclined to evil, and that
continually.

> The Methodist Articles of Religion

We have no-one to blame but ourselves when we
choose to sin. And no one to thank but our Creator
when he chooses to save us from our sins . . . again.

> *Bad Girls of the Bible* (popular Evangelical
> book by Liz Curtis Higgs, 1999)

his divinity signalled by an aura or halo, his power manifest in his bearing (often seated on a throne, with a hand raised in blessing, sometimes with a book of law). He is usually located beyond the mundane world in an empty, dimensionless golden space. We are dealing here with 'icons' rather than portraits – magical images that offer access to the mysterious divine power they represent.

Consider the image of Christ Pantocrator ('Christ the ruler of all things'), which is located high above the altar in some churches in the East (see Fig. 5 overleaf). To see it you look upwards, above the earth and the human condition, where the saviour dwells in heavenly splendour. The architecture and decoration in the churches in which the image is set are deliberately designed to give an impression of heaven brought down to earth. In entering one steps out of the mundane world and into a space that gives a foretaste of the higher and better reality that surrounds it – the world of Jesus, Mary, and the saints. More real than this world, this paradise can be accessed here and now by receiving the church's sacraments, participating in its rituals, hearing its music, viewing its dazzling images, and obeying its authority.

Until the early Middle Ages such images of Christ dominated the Christian imagination. Gradually, however, they were supplemented with something rather different: depictions of Christ suffering and dying – Christ on the cross, Christ being taken down from the cross, and the Pietà (the dead Christ cradled in the arms of his mother Mary). As we will see in later chapters, the change was bound up with new forms of devotion that focused not only on the glory and majesty of the saviour, but on his suffering. Images of Christ's death encouraged believers to meditate on his unique suffering, the sinfulness that nailed him to the cross, and the amazing love of the saviour. As well as signalling Christ's humanity, such images had the effect of underlining his unique divinity (see Fig. 6 on page 33).

5. Christ Pantocrator, Abbey Church of Monreale, Sicily (12th century).

Some of the images produced by the Renaissance of the 14th, 15th, and 16th centuries drew Christ much closer to the human condition. So-called because it involved a re-naissance ('re-birth') of classical culture, this European cultural movement revived the Ancient Greek and Roman theme of the dignity of the human condition. Since it was a Christian as much as a classical movement, this dignity was often expressed by way of images of Jesus. In the

6. Crucifixion, by Matthias Grunewald (1500–8).

work of the early Renaissance artist Giotto, for example, Jesus
appears as human not merely by virtue of his suffering, but in his
ability to feel and express the full range of human emotions by way
of a solid, three-dimensional body of flesh and blood. Even Giotto's
angels have feelings; like Jesus' devoted human followers they
weep and beat their breasts as they behold the death of Christ. Later
Renaissance art would go even further towards the humanization

of Jesus, sometimes depicting him naked and with male genitalia, thereby interpreting even human sexuality as a mark of potential human perfection rather than Fall.

The Reformation of the 16th century brought with it something of a reaction against these more obviously human images of Jesus, and a re-emphasis on his unique relationship with the Almighty Father God. Catholic art found ways of depicting Christ as a supra-human being who exceeds the human condition and dwells in the heavens, whilst Protestant art sometimes conveyed the authority of Christ by picturing him as literally 'backed up' by the Father. In many depictions Christ is removed from the repertoire of the human by being idealized. Both he and the Virgin Mary now appear as ideal types of moral perfection and human beauty, compared to which actual human beings will always fall short. As such, they can have the effect of reinforcing a sense of human sinfulness rather than human potential, whilst appearing on the surface to do the opposite (Fig. 7).

7. *The Holy Family with a Little Bird*, by Murillo (c. 1650).

The tendency of Christian art to depict Jesus as human – only better – continued in the 19th and 20th centuries. With the invention of cheap printing, images of Jesus became more widely available than ever before. The majority depict a handsome man who is both masterful and compassionate. In Roman Catholic depictions of The Sacred Heart (see Fig. 8 on page 36), Jesus literally lays bare his heart to those who would love, or scorn, him. In Holman Hunt's famous allegory *The Light of the World* (see Fig. 9 on page 37), he knocks on the door that symbolizes the human soul and that can only be opened from within. In Warner Sallman's popular portrait of Jesus (see Fig. 10 on page 38) he appears as a handsome, caring all-American male (Sallman rejected an early version with the comment: 'top of hair and head looks feminine'). Such images still speak of Jesus' divinity more than his humanity, for they do more to remove him from the normal human condition than to identify him with it. The 'removal' is obviously greater for women than for men (see Chapter 7).

Promises made by Our Lord Jesus Christ to Blessed Margaret Mary

In favour of those devoted to His Sacred Heart

1. I will give them all the graces necessary for their state.

2. I will put peace in their families.

3. I will console them in all their troubles.

4. I will be their sure refuge during life, and particularly at the hour of death.

5. I will abundantly bless all their enterprises.

6. Sinners shall find in My Heart an infinite ocean of mercy.

7. Faithful souls shall become fervent.

8. Fervent souls shall rise rapidly to a great perfection.

9. I will bless the houses where an image of my Sacred Heart is exposed and honoured.

10. I will give priests the gift of touching the most hardened hearts.

11. Those who propagate this devotion shall have their names written in My Heart, never to be effaced.

12. To those who communicate the first Friday of the month for nine consecutive months, I promise the grace of final repentance; they shall not die in My disfavour, nor without receiving the Sacraments, and My Heart shall be their refuge at that last hour.

Behold this Heart which has loved men so much.

BOUASSE-LEBEL. · 1851. · PARIS

8. The Sacred Heart of Jesus. Image on a popular card (c. 1900).

9. *The Light of the World*, by Holman Hunt (1900–4).

10. *Head of Christ*, by Warner Sallman (1941).

Laying hold of salvation

Christianity developed many different ways of explaining how Christ saves (so-called 'theories of atonement'). Some said he had defeated the devil and his angels, others that he was a sacrifice to God, still others that humans are saved by entering into mystical union with Christ. In modern times the theory of 'substitutionary atonement' has become very influential, especially in Evangelical circles (see Chapter 5). It holds that Christ becomes a substitute for humanity, taking our sins upon himself and suffering the necessary punishment on our behalf.

Behind these different theories was the shared view that we are saved not by anything we do, are, or can achieve, but solely by the initiative of God working through Christ to save us. In the most extreme view, the view of Augustine and some of the Protestant reformers, even when we are saved we remain sinners: God simply chooses not to condemn us for our sins (see Chapter 3). For other Christian thinkers, salvation does effect some change and improvement in the human condition, even if it fails to make us perfect. At the other pole of the spectrum is the minority view that salvation can result in human perfection, even divinization (see Chapters 4 and 5).

Despite their characteristic stress on human passivity in relation to salvation, however, Christian leaders and teachers were clear that there was something Christians could and must do in order to be saved – have faith in God's saving power, and join the church. In Christianity God's grace is mediated to humanity through two channels, 'Word' and 'sacrament', and both are best received by way of a Christian community. Though different forms of Christianity might lay more stress to the one or the other channel of grace, all Christian worship services are composed of some mixture of the two: reading from the Bible, preaching and exposition of the Word, consecration and reception of sacraments.

A sacrament is a material object that symbolizes and transmits divine power. Although the Catholic Church would eventually recognize seven sacraments (baptism, Eucharist, penance, confirmation, ordination, marriage, extreme unction), the two sacraments recognized by all Christian churches are baptism and Eucharist (the latter may also be called 'Mass', 'Holy Communion' or 'the Lord's Supper'). Their basic elements could not be simpler: in baptism, a washing in water; in the Eucharist, a sharing of bread and wine.

Through baptism an individual is 'born again', not into the world but into the church, and not by natural birth but by supernatural re-birth. The transition is marked by an immersion in water, which symbolizes entry into the womb or the grave, as well as a washing and cleansing. Christological significance is expressed through the language of 'washing in the blood of the lamb' (where Christ is likened to a sacrificial lamb), and in the metaphor of a 'dying' of the old life in order to live in Christ. The ritual brings new life in several senses. First, in that one is no longer under the power of the devil and evil spirits but under the Lordship of Christ (a transition that is also marked by anointing with oil after the baptism). Second, that one is living by a new set of standards – not of the world but of God and His church. Third, that one is no longer living the old mortal life but has already begun to live the risen life of Christ – in anticipation of eternal life.

The Eucharist repeats, reiterates, and reinforces the message of baptism. The simple act of sharing a meal has an obvious significance in binding together those who participate. For Christians this significance was extended by virtue of the fact that Christ, at the Last Supper he ate with his disciples, is said to have commanded them to 'do this in remembrance of me'. What is more, the bread and wine can be understood as a symbol of the sacrifice that he then made and the gift he offers: his flesh and blood given for the salvation of the human race. The symbolism is powerful: those who participate are being nourished by Christ's body; his flesh is becoming part of them and they are becoming part of him, whilst also being drawn into closer relationship with one another. Since Christ's death on the cross is often interpreted as a sacrificial offering to God, so the Eucharist can be understood as a symbol or even a repetition of this unique sacrifice of the beloved Son.

11. *Mass of Saint Gregory*, by Israhel van Meckenem (1490s). This engraving commemorates a vision in which Jesus appeared to Pope Gregory the Great (c. 540–604) as he celebrated Mass. Jesus' blood pours into the chalice, while his body represents the bread of the Mass. There could be no more vivid representation of Christian belief in the 'real presence' of the God-man in the sacraments.

Christianity operates, in other words, by taking basic elements of 'natural', unredeemed life and sacralizing them by bringing them into relation with the transforming power of God. It does the same with time, dividing up the calendar not on the basis of nature's seasons and rhythms, but according to the life and death of Christ. Thus the Christian world counts time forwards from the birth of Christ, and organizes the year around Christ's birth (Christmas), his death and resurrection (Good Friday and Easter), and other lesser feasts and fasts. Even the Christian week pivots around the day on which Christ was raised from the dead (Sunday) (see Figure 13, page 60). By hearing God's Word, and by receiving the sacraments, individual life, social life – indeed the whole of creation – is conformed ever more closely to the higher power of God, revealed in the life, death, and resurrection of the God-man.

Spirit and world

The characteristic Christian framework of sin and salvation abases the human and exalts the divine. The good life is not the life lived according to one's deepest instincts and desires, but the life lived according to the higher standards of God as witnessed to by Christ. One must destroy and give up one's own will and appetites in order to live wholly according to the pattern of Christ. Thus God, the saviour and the means of salvation – Word and sacraments – are all 'objective' and external to the believer. One is saved not by what lies within, but by what lies outside and is in a significant sense alien to the human condition.

This outward and objective orientation is qualified, however, by Christian belief in the Holy Spirit. God the Father dwells above in the heavens, and His Son sits on his right hand. But not only did His Son come down to earth to save us, He is still present and accessible on earth by way of His Spirit. In Christian thought, the Spirit is inseparable from Father and Son; 'He' is the Spirit *of* God and the Spirit *of* Christ. Rather than existing above the world, the Spirit is God's presence in the world – and in the heart of the believer. In other words, the Spirit qualifies Christian belief in the transcendent otherness of God, and brings the divine *into* life. And the greater the emphasis that Christians and Christian groups place upon the Spirit, the more they shift the focus of their religion from higher power to power within.

Even the 'highest' forms of Christianity believe in the Holy Spirit, at least in theory, but the Spirit has played a less prominent role in orthodox Christian life and thought than God the Father and God the Son. The New Testament has no systematic doctrine of the Spirit ('pneumatology'). The Holy Spirit descends upon Jesus 'as a dove' when Jesus is baptized in the River Jordan by John the Baptist; it 'overshadows' Mary when she conceives Jesus; and it is poured out on Christ's followers after he ascends to heaven (at Pentecost). For Paul the Spirit takes possession of Christians at baptism, taking the place of the evil spirits who formerly enslaved them, and filling them instead with the mind and life of Christ. It was several centuries before orthodox Christianity arrived at an agreement that the Holy Spirit was divine in the same way and to the same degree as the Father and the Son. Even then the Spirit was defined as 'proceeding' or being 'breathed' from the Father, which suggested that the Spirit was in some way subject to the higher authority of the Father. This impression was reinforced when, after the 6th century, the Western churches began to affirm that the Holy Spirit 'proceeds from the Father *and* the Son' (see Chapter 6). The effect, on the imagination at least, was to subordinate Spirit to Father and Son, just as the effect of liturgical practice was to subordinate it to Word and sacrament.

But the Spirit remains the rogue element in Christianity, the sacred in a form that is hardest for the churches to pin down and control. Despite the precautions that have been taken, it is always open to ordinary women and men to claim its inspiration and, in doing so, to lay hold of God's own power for themselves. Although Christianity took pains to identify divine power with its own institutions, rituals, sacraments, and scriptures exclusively, the

Spirit may be received as a free-floating divine power which anyone can plug into – without the authorization of the church or the need for its mediating agency. As we will see in Chapter 4, radical Christian groups such as the Quakers who developed a very high doctrine of the Spirit dispensed with priests, scriptures, and sacraments altogether. They had no need of these external containers of the divine when, in their view, the sacred could enter directly into human life.

Not only may the Spirit challenge the Christian preference for higher power, it can also qualify a general Christian preference for stability and changelessness. The Christian God is normally said to be changeless. He brings into being a world that is fully formed. Christ has been at the right hand of God from all eternity. The end will be like the beginning – paradise will be restored and the second Adam will take the place set aside for him from all eternity. The truth has been laid out in Christ's revelation once and for all. The best that can be hoped for is recapitulation, restoration, and reformation. These are common, and central, themes in Christian life and thought. By contrast, the Spirit highlights a different, more suppressed theme in Christianity: that the divine is present in and through change, working to 'make all things new'.

This is not to imply that Christianity is generally content with the world in which it finds itself. Far from it. In looking above, Christianity also looks beyond. It cherishes and nourishes a vision of perfection – not the way things are but the way they ought to be. The vision is summed up in Christ, and is nurtured, enacted, and embodied in the ritual actions that Christians perform as they come together to worship. Such ritual always anticipates what lies beyond. Such 'beyondness' may be thought of in spatial terms as 'up there' (heaven, higher than the world) or in temporal terms as 'to come' (the coming Kingdom of God, the end of the world, the return of Jesus). Consequently, Christianity says both that individuals go to heaven when they die, and that they will be resurrected at the end of time – and Christian ritual and expectation looks forward to both.

For Christians of all hues, then, this world is not the only – nor the best – world. There is something higher that must be aspired to, and something better that can be hoped for. The consequences of this belief are varied. For some, it means rejecting this world, this life, this body in order to prepare for the higher life that is to come (the ascetic tendency). For others, it means 'treading lightly' in the world: taking its joys and satisfactions, sufferings and frustrations as transitory and relatively insubstantial compared to the life to come. And for some the vision of perfection acts as a provocation to act in the world here and now in order to bring it more closely into line with God's higher standards. Belief in the Spirit can inspire each and every one of these options.

Conclusion

What sets Christianity apart from other monotheisms and turns it into a religion in its own right is its emphasis on the unique God-man in whom the might, majesty, and mercy of God are made visible and accessible to mortals. This saviour becomes the focus of a new community of worship (the church) with distinctive beliefs and rituals. Its promise is that all who join, receive its sacraments, and hear its Word, will be saved from sin and death and admitted into the kingdom of heaven. Emphasis on the higher power of God is, however, qualified by Christian belief in the Holy Spirit – in the divine as it comes within human life rather than standing over and above it.

Chapter 3
Church and Biblical Christianity

This chapter considers in more detail how a mode of Christianity orientated around higher power became dominant. Covering the period from the 4th century to the dawn of the modern period, it traces the development of the two most important manifestations of such Christianity – what can be called 'Church Christianity' and 'Biblical Christianity'. Church Christianity has had the most extensive influence over the longest period of all types of Christianity. Both the Roman Catholic Church and the Eastern Orthodox Church belong to this type, as do many of the earlier Protestant churches, most notably the Lutheran, Presbyterian, and Anglican churches (see below). With its origins in the upheavals of the Protestant Reformation of the 16th century, Biblical Christianity develops out of Church Christianity, and retains a number of its characteristics, including its orientation around higher power. But instead of locating such power – on earth – in the church, its rituals and traditions, priests and sacraments, it attributes highest authority to the Bible.

Characteristics of Church Christianity

The fact that the word 'church' refers both to a community of Christians and the building in which they gather is not inconsequential, for this style of building, first developed by Church Christianity, tells us a good deal about the latter's characteristic commitments.

One obvious thing about a church is that its main space is designed to accommodate a group of people. Unlike many temples, or meditation rooms, a church is not designed primarily for individuals coming into the presence of the sacred on a one-to-one basis, but for a group coming into the presence of God. Yet the group is not itself the main focus of what goes on in these buildings. If the purpose were simply for people to meet one another, churches could look like meeting halls. Instead, they tend to be tall, impressive, imposing buildings. The interior space usually rises to the rafters, whilst from outside the impression of height is accentuated by a tower or steeple. The effect is to draw attention away from the self and the group towards that which transcends them – an effect which is heightened when walls, windows, and ceilings are decorated with images of the heavens and their inhabitants. The design carries a message: that such religion looks to a God who is higher than human beings and who calls forth their worship, praise, obedience, service, obeisance. (Hence the name of the main activity for which these buildings are constructed: 'worship service'.)

As well as directing attention upwards, churches direct it towards a focal point at the east end of the building, where an altar is located (most churches are rectangular, with the longest sides of the rectangle running east to west). A font, designed to contain water for baptism, may also be prominent somewhere in the building. Taken in combination with the 'vertical' focus on transcendence, the effect is to suggest that even though God may dwell high above in the heavens, He is available here on earth by way of the church's sacraments – the bread and wine of the Eucharist, the water of baptism. This sacramental focus is a key characteristic of Church Christianity. Though it reveres the Bible, its architecture tells us that it gives a still more important place to the sacraments, for the pulpit is rarely in as prominent a place as the altar.

Sacramentalism goes hand in hand with another key characteristic of Church Christianity: sacerdotalism (the granting of authority to an ordained 'clergy' who are set apart from the 'laity'). The two characteristics go hand in hand, because sacraments require priests to consecrate and administer them, and the power of the one reinforces the power of the other. If it is believed that the bread and wine of the Eucharist are really the body and blood of the God-man, then the men who handle them are the deputies of God Himself, with divine power in their hands. What is more, since you can only have a sacrament if you have a priest (since he alone is allowed to perform the rituals in which the elements of water, bread, and wine are transformed into sacred objects), and since you can only have a church if you have the sacraments, there can be no living church without a clergyman.

At the very heart of Church Christianity, then, there is a hierarchical power that flows down from heaven to earth. At the top of the pyramid is God the Father, in whom all power is concentrated. His power is mediated by His Son, Jesus Christ, who, in turn, channels power through his designated representatives on earth, the clergy. Thus Church Christianity structures its own life – the life of God's people – after the hierarchical model of divine power from on high. What is more, it extends this model to the whole of society. In Church Christianity the belief that Christ is Lord of all the earth engenders a sense of responsibility not only for those already inside the church, but for those outside. In order to discharge this responsibility, it is willing to work with the wider society. Thus Church Christianity aims to create a universal Christian society, and when opportunity presents itself, it is willing to enter into alliance with political power to achieve this aim.

Origins of Church Christianity

It is quite possible that Jesus envisaged a fully egalitarian society whose members share table fellowship, teach and minister to one another, and refuse to acknowledge any authority except that of a God of Love. How did a movement inspired by such ideals turn into a hierarchical, sacramental, sacerdotal church?

We can glimpse a transitional stage in the process in the communities to which Paul writes. Authority within these groups is conferred according to particular gifts bestowed on people by the Holy Spirit – such as preaching, teaching, prophecy, and healing. But it is clear that a few individuals, including Paul himself, are trying to claim special authority for themselves, an authority that is justified in terms of their direct contact with the risen Lord (whom Paul has encountered in a rapture). Although egalitarian, Spirit-led forms of Christian community would continue to exist (see the next chapter), they appear to have been challenged by those who believed that order and unity could be achieved by way of hierarchical leadership.

As formal leadership roles developed, they were reserved for men and, amongst men, for those who could claim some direct association with Jesus. As time went by and Jesus' contemporaries began to die off, the idea of 'apostolic succession' developed, according to which authority was passed down a male line that could be traced back to Jesus and the 'apostles' who had known him directly. In order to make sure that the purity of this line was safeguarded, those who belonged to it chose their successors carefully, and authorized them through a laying on of hands, which gradually developed into a formal rite of priestly 'ordination'. Leaders were not simply chosen by the community; they were ordained by God, and set apart from the rest of humanity.

As well as concentrating power in the hands of a few, apostolic succession helped secure uniformity of belief amongst Christians. Although 'heretics' might claim to know the wisdom of Jesus by direct inspiration, their 'orthodox' opponents could claim to be more faithful to the memory of what the historical Jesus actually said and did – since they stood in a chain of received wisdom that stretched back to him. Apostolic succession was equally important as a way of tying a developing sacramentalism to the office of a recognized priesthood. In Jewish and Graeco-Roman religion, a

49

priest was normally a person authorized to perform sacrifice, and hence to stand between the humans who offered the sacrifice and the God who received it. As Christianity developed an understanding of Christ's death as sacrifice and the Eucharist as a repetition of this once-for-all offering, so the language of priesthood became more appropriate. Christian priests were understood to stand in a special relation to the God-man by virtue not only of apostolic succession, but because of their ability to offer His sacrifice at the altar on behalf of the people. One reason the priestly office was reserved for men was because it was thought more appropriate for a male to represent the God-man than for a female to do so (see Chapter 7).

By the 2nd century all these lines of development were coming together to form the basis of Church Christianity. Its advocates preferred to speak of it as 'catholic' which means 'universal', or 'orthodox' which means 'true belief'. By presenting itself as the one true, universal form of Christianity, it was possible to make alternative versions of the faith look like deviations from a pure root stock and their followers like schismatics and heretics. But the claim to catholicity also had a strong institutional underpinning, given that Church Christianity had established a clear line of leadership, a unified set of ritual practices and a unifying focus in the only Son of the One True God. The drive towards unity was reinforced by the establishment of a hierarchy of leadership in which 'bishops' oversaw 'priests', who in turn had authority over 'deacons' (responsible for pastoral care and other services) and lay people. All these developments helped enforce discipline within Church Christianity and bind many separate communities together under a single 'head', Jesus Christ, represented on earth by the bishop.

As well as being marked by orderliness and hierarchy, Church Christianity was characterized by social conservatism. Its representatives had little desire to rock the boat of the Graeco-Roman urban society in which they were now situated

Extract from Ignatius, to the Smyreans

The letters of Ignatius (c. 35–c. 107) provide an early glimpse of a Christian leader striving to establish episcopal authority (the leadership of bishops) by arguing that the hierarchy of heaven must be reflected within the organization of the church.

> Avoid divisions, as the beginning of evil. Follow, all of you, the bishop, as Jesus Christ followed the Father . . . Let that eucharist be considered valid which is under the bishop or him to whom he commits it . . . Whatsover [the bishop] approves, that is well pleasing to God.

(the Jesus movement's roots in rural, peasant society had been quickly left behind). True, Christians liked to draw a distinction between the sexual licence and immorality that characterized wider society and their own commitment to chastity and life-long marriage, but many respectable Romans would have been sympathetic to such a chaste sexual ethic. When it came to more radical matters such as questioning the patriarchal nature of the family, masculine domination in general, or the slave-based economy of the Roman Empire, Church Christianity was silent. Its apologists were more concerned to convince the Romans that Christians were trustworthy, moral, and loyal citizens whose presence in the Empire could only serve to strengthen it.

But there was one area where Church Christians would not compromise, however much offence it caused. Christians insisted that theirs was the only true God, that He demanded exclusive loyalty, that other so-called gods were demons and evil spirits, and that only by accepting the God of Jesus Christ could people be saved. Such exclusivism troubled the Romans, who were tolerant of religions throughout the Empire so long as they, in turn, were tolerant of one another. The Christians' refusal to honour the Roman gods was considered a political as well as a religious offence, for the strength of the Empire was believed to depend upon the proper observance of its religion. When imperial decrees demanded sacrifice to the Roman gods, some Christians refused. To the Romans' amazement, a significant number demonstrated their willingness to die rather than betray their God for an 'idol', thus becoming the first Christian martyrs.

Empire and church

Despite its institutional strength and unity, and the powerful witness of martyrdom, Church Christianity's rise to power would probably never have come about had the Roman Emperor himself not converted to its cause.

Prior to the year 313, in which the Emperor Constantine promulgated the famous Edict of Milan granting toleration to all religions in the Empire, Church Christianity faced dangers on every side. As we will see in the next chapter, it was engaged in a life-and-death struggle with rival forms of Christianity, a struggle whose outcome was far from certain. What is more, it suffered from sporadic but sometimes deadly forms of persecution by the Romans, some of whom had the support of a provincial ruler or even the Emperor himself. Such persecution might result not only in loss of life, but in confiscation of money, property, and books.

There is, however, far more to the story of the Empire's relation to Church Christianity than persecution, for there were many Romans who were sympathetic to this new religion, and a good number who joined it. What is more, Church Christianity appears to have been particularly successful within the capital of the Empire, Rome, and to have attracted some noble and high-born Romans to its ranks. Since it did not disrupt Roman life and institutions too greatly, other than by calling for a more rigorous personal morality and an abandonment of all other forms of worship, this is not as surprising as it might appear.

Nor is it so surprising that a Roman Emperor might see the advantages of Church Christianity not only for himself but for his Empire. This, after all, was a religion that understood power as the possession of an Almighty God on high, not of the people below. Far better that the Emperor be understood as God's deputy on earth, upholding divine justice, than as a tyrant whose position was based on force. Far better too that his people acknowledge his divine right to rule, and their own duty to submit to him, a sacred obligation. What is more, Christianity might help an ambitious Emperor achieve his dream of unifiying and extending the Empire; for the church also cherished dreams of universal conquest – of souls at least.

It was not only the Emperor who saw advantages in a church-state alliance. Church Christianity willingly accepted imperial patronage because it too had a great deal to gain. In the ancient world religions without political backing were always vulnerable and exposed. Once Constantine and his successors threw their weight behind the church, its success was virtually assured. Not only did it win enormous financial and legal advantages, but bishops could now call upon the might of the state to oppose their rivals: competing forms of Christianity ('heresy') and Hellenistic religion and culture ('paganism'). The bishop became a figure of considerable temporal as well as spiritual power in his diocese (an area of jurisdiction modelled on a unit of imperial administration), and a representative of the earthly as well as the heavenly ruler. Perhaps most important of all, Christianity's claim to speak on behalf of the Almighty God gained new plausibility. Christian writers like Eusebius of Caesarea (c. 260–c. 340) were quick to characterize Constantine as 'the deputy of Christ', and eager to insist that the alliance of church and Empire was part of God's providential plan for the world.

Extract from Eusebius, Oration, 3.5–6

Invested as he is with a semblance of heavenly sovereignty, [the Emperor] directs his gaze above, and frames his earthly rule according to the pattern of the divine original, feeling strength in its conformity to the monarchy of God ... And surely monarchy far transcends every other constitution and form of government: for that democratic equality of power, which is its opposite, may rather be described as anarchy and disorder.

Doctrinal division

Though Constantine was attracted by the church's drive to achieve unity, he would soon become aware of its ability to provoke disunity. Not only was Church Christianity in the 4th century struggling to defeat alternative versions of Christianity, it was also being shaken by division within its own ranks. Although personal and political rivalries between different cities, regions, and bishops played an important role in these disputes, they came to a focus over a doctrinal issue: the status of Jesus.

Matters came to a head in Constantine's day because of the growing popularity of the views of Arius (d. 366), a presbyter from Alexandria in Egypt. Arius proposed that Jesus should be understood neither as God nor man, but as a quasi-divine being whose status hovered somewhere between the two. He argued that Jesus was created by the Father and that there was therefore a time 'when he was not'. Consequently, the Son must be of lesser status than the Father. Although the Arian position gained significant Christian support, some, like Athanasius of Alexandria (c. 296–373), realized that it undermined the very basis of the church. If Jesus were not truly God and truly human, he would not be able to assume human nature and save it by bringing it within the scope of divinity. Christianity would be a second-rate religion that put human beings in touch not with the exclusive mediator between God and man, but with a middle-ranking deity. Its sacraments, priesthood, and church would lose power as a result.

So serious was this dispute that in 325 Constantine called a council at Nicaea, in present-day Turkey, in order to settle it. Bishops assembled and learned men gave their views. In the end, the opinion of Athanasius and his supporters won the day and Arius was anathematized. The council drew up one of the most influential and widely accepted Christian creeds (statements of belief): the Creed of Nicaea. Its key clause stated that Jesus was 'homoousios': from the Greek, of one (homo) substance (ousios) with the Father. In other words, Jesus shared the very essence of divinity.

Extract from the Nicaean Creed (325 CE)

We believe in One God, the Father, Almighty . . .
And in One Lord Jesus Christ, the Son of God,
    begotten of the Father, Only-begotten, that is, from
    the substance of the Father;
God from God, Light from Light, Very God from Very
    God . . .
And those who say 'There was when he was not' . . .
    The Catholic and Apostolic church anathematizes.

Arianism did not die out overnight, not least because it was adopted by some of the so-called barbarian tribes on the fringes of the Empire. But the Council of Nicaea was nevertheless the most successful of the many subsequent councils that would be called to settle other contentious points of doctrine and church order. Later councils found it increasingly difficult to establish unity. The influential Council of Chalcedon of 451, for example, clarified what had been implied at Nicaea by saying that Jesus was 'very God and very man', but failed to win the same widespread assent. As we will see in Chapter 6, two large portions of the church split from the 'catholic' church after Chalcedon: the Nestorian churches of Antioch, Persia, and further east; and the Monophysite churches of North Africa and Syria (remnants of which still exist). By requiring credal conformity on the part of all its members, Church Christianity had managed to maintain unity, but had alienated large parts of its constituency.

Christendom

The alliance of church and empire survived for over a thousand years, and shaped both partners in the process. The Empire that had had its capital in Rome and its cultural heart in the classical world gradually gave way to a more Christian version. In 330 Constantine moved his capital to Byzantium or 'Constantinople' (now Istanbul), and the Empire slowly changed both its name and its nature to become the 'Byzantine Empire' (though its citizens would still call themselves 'Romans'). The shift of power eastwards accelerated after the 4th century when barbarian tribes from north-eastern Europe, pushing south and west in search of new land and wealth, conquered much of the western part of the Empire, including Rome.

Given its status as the right arm of empire, Church Christianity in the East (which eventually became known as Eastern Orthodoxy, see Chapter 6) looked back on the beleaguered churches in the West with sympathy and condescension. With the Empire collapsing around it, Christianity in the West found itself exposed, without secular power to fall back on. Before long, however, it would begin to turn such apparently adverse circumstances to its advantage. What could have been a disaster became an opportunity as the Western church and clergy began to move into the vacuum created by the collapse of Roman power.

12. Sacred power dignifies secular power: an ivory relief from Constantinople depicts Christ himself crowning the co-Emperor of the Byzantine Empire, Romanus II, and his wife, Eudocia (945–9).

Whereas the Greek-speaking church in the East remained under the control of the political ruler, the Latin-speaking church in the West found itself in a position to take control of political affairs itself – if not directly, then by exercising control over earthly rulers. One reason the church in the West was able to do this was that power was now shared between so many competing warrior kings, princes, and prince-bishops that no single ruler was ever able to become dominant for long. With its ancient credentials and base in Rome, its widely distributed communities and effective infrastructure, its growing wealth and lands, the church had become an important power in its own right. Successive bishops of Rome were quick to take advantage and to claim leadership over the whole Western church; by the late 6th century they were being called 'pope' – 'father' of the church.

By the early Middle Ages, the pope was even beginning to challenge the power of the patriarch in the East. No serious ruler in the West could now afford to ignore him. He had the power to legitimate those who supported him and to excommunicate those who did not (excommunication not only cut a ruler off from the church, its sacraments, and salvation, but gave his people licence to disobey him). Thus was born the dream of 'Christendom', of a unified Christian society under the ultimate control of the pope and the church and protected by secular leaders who respected the authority of Rome. By anointing the most powerful dynastic leaders in Europe (including Charlemagne in 800), the popes tried to establish a new line of Holy Roman emperors in the West who would do their bidding. In practice, however, the religio-political ideal of an orderly hierarchy of power flowing from God to Christ to pope to Holy Roman emperor was continually disrupted as secular leaders competed with the papacy for political ascendancy. The balance of power was such that neither side was ever dominant for long, and the struggle would continue throughout the medieval period and beyond.

Even though the church never managed to win decisive control over secular affairs, it did manage to establish itself, and Christian culture, throughout most of Western Europe – and thus to unify the whole region (without the church, there would be no 'Europe'). In late antiquity and the early Middle Ages, evangelization (the spread of Christianity) generally took place from the top down. When a non-Christian ruler was converted to Church Christianity (sometimes from 'paganism', sometimes from a 'heretical' form of Christianity like Arianism), he would have his household and people baptized as well. Gradually monasteries and churches would be established in his realm, often through the patronage of the ruler and wealthy landowners, and a more profound contact with the Christian message and way of life might be brought about as a result. The colonization of Europe by stone-built churches and cathedrals took place during the Middle Ages, and by the end of this period nearly every man, woman, and child would be securely located within the 'parish' of a local church and the 'diocese' of a cathedral and its bishop. Bit by bit the Christian world view, its God and its saints, its leaders and institutions, displaced the more ancient religions and cults of Europe, and established Christianity as the 'truth' into which the people of Europe would be born and baptized.

By the high Middle Ages, Church Christianty's dream of a unified Christian society had come closer to being realized than at any time before or since. Because this society was based on unity of belief and practice, any deviation had either to be assimilated or destroyed, lest it threaten not only the church but the whole social order. The medieval church expended a good deal of energy in protecting itself not only against external threats like 'the Turk' (the symbol of the steadily growing power of Islamic civilization), but internal threats as well. The Jews were one group that proved particularly problematic because of their ambivalent status as highly educated and literate worshippers of the one true God who nevertheless rejected Christ and his church. As a potential 'enemy within' they were alternately tolerated, employed, admired, and persecuted. Much energy was also devoted to identifying,

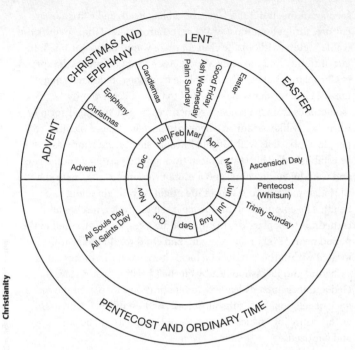

13. The Christian year.

classifying, and rooting out 'heresy' – beliefs and practices that
deviated from the church norm. Secular rulers cooperated with
the church in attacking popular heretical movements such as
Catharism (also called Albigensianism) with the sword as well as
with preaching and, by the later Middle Ages, with organized
'inquisitions'.

As we will see in the next chapter, many of the heretical movements
that challenged Christianity from within opposed the church's
wealth and power with the ideal of Christ-like poverty and
powerlessness. This upsurge of internal protest reminds us that
despite its orientation around higher power, it was impossible for
Church Christianity openly to seek dominating power for its own

14. A symbol of the victory of Catholic orthodoxy over Albigensian heresy, the cathedral in Albi, southern France (1277–1512), serves as a reminder of the dominating power of the church that built it.

sake, or to maintain that 'might is right'. For one thing, Christianity contained an internal check on the exercise of tyrannical power in its view that God – though omnipotent – exercises power in a paternal way, seeking the best for His 'children'. For another, Christians worshipped a God-man who had refused to exercise dominating power, and had died helpless on a cross. Those who followed Him were called to serve rather than to command, and to sacrifice rather than accumulate. Even as they sought to extend the power of the church, Christian leaders had therefore to be careful to exercise this power in a benevolent and paternalistic fashion – and to make sure that the political rulers with whom they allied themselves did the same. Even then, some Christians remained critical of the church's pursuit of power. By the later Middle Ages, calls for a reform of the church 'in head and members' were becoming common. The standing of the papacy was further threatened by a series of disastrous confrontations and disputes with secular power, which led both to the 'exile' of the papacy in Avignon, France, and to a papal schism which saw two – and at one point three – rivals all claiming to be Pope.

Thomas Aquinas and Scholasticism

'Scholasticism' was the theological project that accompanied Christendom, and attempted to organize all existing knowledge, both Christian and Graeco-Roman, into a single system. This system would provide a unified intellectual account of all things – God, man, and the world. Scholasticism proceeded by a distinctive method: asking a question, considering texts that had a bearing upon it, deliberating about their overall conclusion, and arriving at an answer – before proceeding to the next question. It was a 'science' that could be undertaken by only the most learned men of the period, and the greatest of them became highly celebrated. Thomas Aquinas (c. 1225–74) constructed an extensive and influential system of scholastic theology in his massive *Summa Theologiae*. His project is sometimes referred to as 'scholastic humanism' because of the relatively positive view it took of human nature and human reason. Aquinas believed that 'nature must be perfected by grace', and did not understand it to be totally corrupted by sin. Aquinas was made the official theologian of the Roman Catholic Church several centuries after his death.

The Protestant Reformation

The challenges faced by Church Christianity – at the very height of its power – were bound up with social change. By the 11th century the shape of Western society was beginning to change quite fundamentally. Wealth derived from improved agricultural yields gave rise to a market for manufactured goods, which in turn supported the rise of a new class of artisans and manufacturers. As more people were freed from the land, they moved into the rapidly expanding towns and cities. The latter posed a threat to the church, for they were much harder to control than rural areas, ideas could spread more quickly, and the newly wealthy classes who made up part of their population were increasingly eager to seize the church's power for themselves.

In the 13th century a new wave of enthusiasm for the 'apostolic life' of simplicity and poverty swept across Europe and found institutional expression in the formation of new orders of 'friars' or 'mendicants' (see next chapter). Lay movements of pious women also began to develop. At first the church weathered this storm by giving its blessing to the friars and some other advocates of vowed poverty and by harnessing their energies to serve its own ends, including the attack on heresy. By the 15th and 16th centuries, however, the call for church reform was taking forms that were harder for the church to neutralize or assimilate, and the result would be the first major division of orthodoxy since West and East had drifted apart (although the latter split is sometimes dated to the 'Photian schism' of 836–7 and the mutual anathemas of 1054, it began much earlier and became irrevocable only much later – see Chapter 6).

The 'Protestant Reformation', as it would come to be called, had several distinctive ingredients. The first was a base in a 'Germany' which was not yet a nation, but a grouping of independent German-speaking political units, some ruled by princes who were eager to take over the church's wealth and power for themselves. The second was a base of support in the towns and cities, some of which were self-governing, and many of which were as impatient with church privilege as the princes. The third was the combination of a charismatic leader, Martin Luther (1483–1546), and the invention of the printing press to disseminate his ideas quickly and relatively cheaply. Printing also made it possible for the Bible to be put into the hands of increasing numbers of men and women and taken out of the church's exclusive control. The final ingredient was theological: Luther's revival of an Augustinian reading of the Bible that emphasized the power of God, the sinfulness of man, and humanity's desperate need of God's salvation wrought by the unique work of Christ.

Even though Luther had originally called for reform not schism, the papacy's unwillingness to accede to any of his demands set him on a collision course with the church of which he had once been a loyal member. After his excommunication by the Pope in 1521, Luther became the leader of a new church which, though it still conformed to the model of Church Christianity, cut itself loose from papal control and abandoned some existing ecclesiastical beliefs and practices. Before long, such Christianity came to be called 'Protestant' in distinction to the 'Catholic' (or 'Roman Catholic') Church based in Rome. Both versions of Christianity regarded themselves as the true church of Christ, and each condemned the other as guilty of straying from God's truth.

In its attitude to power, Protestantism embodied a paradox. On the one hand, it had what might today be labelled democratic tendencies, in that it called for power to be taken out of the hands of the pope and the clergy and delivered back to ordinary Christian men and women. One of its slogans was 'the priesthood of all believers', and one of its central beliefs was that God's Word, embodied in the Bible, should be made more widely available. Since Protestantism gave as much authority to Word as to sacrament, this move encouraged a transfer of power from clergy to people. On the

Luther and Calvin

Whereas the scholastic humanism of Aquinas considered human beings sufficiently free and rational to accept or reject God's grace, Martin Luther became disillusioned with what he regarded as the Catholic Church's over-optimistic view of human capability. His theological disagreement was precipitated by reading Paul and Augustine, who convinced him that human beings could be justified (saved) not by their own works but only by laying hold of God's grace by personal faith. As he puts it:

> The proper subject of theology is man guilty of sin and condemned, and God the Justifier and Saviour of man the sinner. Whatsoever is asked or discussed in theology outside this subject is error and poison.
>
> (Luther, *Works*)

John Calvin (1509–64) was a younger contemporary of Luther who regarded himself as a faithful disciple and interpreter of the senior reformer. In his *Institutes* Calvin gave systematic theological and ethical expression to many of Luther's ideas whilst also moving beyond them in subtle but important respects. For Luther, the best that a human being could hope for was to be justified in spite of sinfulness. Whilst agreeing that we are saved only by grace, Calvin places more emphasis on the value, significance, and effectiveness of morality and law – not only as a reminder of sin, but as the basis of Godly life and society. He set about creating a Godly society in Geneva, a self-governing city that he attempted to organize around strict Christian principles and laws. As Calvin explains his point of view:

> He is said to be justified in God's sight who is both reckoned righteous in God's judgement and has been accepted on account of his righteousness ... wherever there is sin, there also the wrath and vengeance of God show themselves.
>
> (Calvin, *Institutes of the Christian Religion*)

other hand, Reformation theology stressed the absolute sinfulness and powerlessness of humanity and the need for total surrender to an all-powerful Father God and His only Son Jesus Christ. Indeed, Protestantism placed far more emphasis on human depravity and need of grace than medieval Catholic theology. Likewise, it abolished all the mediating beings of medieval Christianity – Mary and the saints – who had stood between earth and heaven and lessened the distance between God and humanity.

In the event, Protestantism transferred power not so much to ordinary people but to the emerging powers in Europe: to national leaders, to the new 'bourgeoisie', to a new order of clergymen or 'pastors', and to men in general rather than to women. Its emphasis on 'liberty' might have awakened the hopes and ambitions of many Christian people, including women and the urban and rural poor, but its equally strong emphasis on the necessity of total submission to the Father and the Son allowed the maintenance of a social order that was still based on the rule of 'fathers': the prince, the magistrate, the feudal lord, the clergyman, the fathers of households, and the masters of the new workshops.

Biblical Christianity

The two denominations that came into existence at the Reformation were the Lutheran Church and the Reformed or Presbyterian Church. The former looked to Martin Luther as its founder, the latter to John Calvin. Despite the important differences between these new Protestant denominations and the Roman Catholic Church, all three exemplified the main characteristics of Church Christianity outlined at the start of this chapter – including the desire to cooperate with secular power in order to bring the whole of society in line with Christian principles. Both the Lutheran and Presbyterian churches quickly formed alliances with state power.

15. Interior of St Mary at Hill, City of London, by Sir Christopher Wren (built 1670–6). The interior of Protestant churches often reflects an emphasis on Word as well as sacrament. Here, the pulpit is prominent and sacred texts (the Ten Commandments, Lord's Prayer, and Apostles' Creed) are displayed on the east wall.

But the Reformation also gave rise to a whole new type of Christianity that may be termed 'Biblical' because of its belief that the Bible is of greater authority than the church, its sacraments and priests, and its desire that the whole of life should be governed by strict conformity to Biblical teaching. Rather than entering into alliance with politics, Biblical Christianity tried to separate itself from 'the world' in order to maintain strict obedience to the uncompromising demands of the Bible.

Biblical Christianity only really made sense in an era in which printing and translation were making the Bible widely available and accessible (in the Roman Catholic Church it was still read by clergy to the people in Latin). With the Bible as the supreme authority in life, Christians needed no other mediator with God – no priest, no bishop, no pope, no theologian. They could form their own communities of 'the saints', all of whom were equal before God since all strove to live in strict conformity to his Word. Since the Bible was often read as endorsing male leadership, women might still be placed under the authority of men, but there was some variety of practice within different Biblical churches.

Once it was accepted that each individual had the right to interpret God's word for himself (and sometimes herself), it became much harder to maintain church unity. Biblical Christianity became notorious for its schisms, since any man was free to set up his own church under his own leadership – on the grounds that this new church would be based on stricter conformity to the Word of God than existing churches. The earliest Biblical churches were lumped together by their Protestant opponents – including Luther and Calvin – as 'Anabaptist', because many of them insisted on adult baptism (on the grounds that it was Biblical and that Christian faith should be voluntary rather than involuntary).

From these early roots developed a number of early Biblical churches, including the Mennonites and Baptists. Their growth and spread was greatly inhibited by the active persecution they faced right across Europe. Such persecution was the product of the new church-state alliances that had been made in the immediate aftermath of the Reformation, when every major political power had allied itself with either a Protestant or Roman Catholic denomination. After a long period of religio-political unrest and war, the religious map of Europe was finally stabilized by the Peace of Westphalia of 1648. Since the unity of both church and state in a particular territory was threatened by the existence of alternative forms of Christianity, 'schismatic' or 'dissenting' churches of all kinds had to be vigorously suppressed, and many Biblical churches were forced into exile on the eastern margins of Europe and later in North America.

The marginalization of Biblical Christianity was reinforced by its theological preference for the total separation of church and state. Unlike Church Christianity, Biblical Christians maintained that

Christian communities should have as little contact with wider society and politics as possible. They believed that faith should be chosen rather than imposed, and should be kept alive in pure communities of the saints living in strict obedience to Jesus' teachings. Since they took Jesus at his word, Biblical Christians often opposed violence in any form, refused to bear arms or swear oaths (including oaths of loyalty to a sovereign), and practised common ownership. They attacked and despised the worldliness of Church Christianity and, although they retained belief in a God of higher power, they preferred to worship Him 'in spirit and in truth' rather than with shows of outward pomp and magnificence.

Conclusion

Christian belief in a hierarchy of power, flowing down from the Father to the Son and thence to the bishop and other clergy, provided a strong foundation on which to build a unified church. A virtuous cycle ensued, for the success of the hierarchical church helped reinforce the plausibility of the celestial hierarchy it was said to mirror, and devotion to God above helped reinforce the authority of the church. Perhaps the most decisive factor of all in the success of Church Christianity, however, was the way in which political rulers – from the Emperor Constantine onwards – found that Christian hierarchical power could guide, assist, and legitimate their own exercise of power. The church could strengthen a ruler's hand by proclaiming him Christ's deputy on earth, whilst a ruler could strengthen the church by giving it his patronage. Thus religious and political power entered into an alliance which endured, in many different guises, right through to the modern period, and whose general effect was to strengthen the hierarchical tendencies of both.

But there is a twist to the tale. Although Christianity was capable of endorsing the exercise of dominating and even tyrannical (masculine) power in both church and state, its repertoire of signs and symbols also favoured something rather different. In so far as God the Father supplied Christians with a model of higher authority, popes, bishops, and kings strove to exercise power with paternal benevolence rather than brute force. In so far as God the Son supplied another model, the consequences could be more radical. Given that the Jesus of gospels steadfastly refused to exercise political power and died powerless at the hands of religious and political authority, some Christians believed that the church should be more eager to renounce wealth and power than to accumulate them. This was the conclusion towards which some Church and Biblical Christians began to be drawn – even though the former resisted the most radical calls for the church to renounce power, and the latter subjected its members to the higher power of the Bible and authorized preachers and pastors. As we will see in the next chapter, there were other Christians who were prepared to go even further, by embracing the idea that God's power can not only command from outside, but inspire from within.

Chapter 4
Mystical Christianity

Whereas the previous chapter considered the development of the main types of Christianity orientated around higher power, this chapter looks at the development of a type of Christianity that is more orientated around power from within, and which may be referred to as 'Mystical Christianity'. Though God may still be worshipped as Father and Son, the Holy Spirit is more likely to be prominent in mystical forms of Christianity. And though the Christian mystic may agree that God is revealed in the externals of church life and teaching, he or she also seeks the divine in the depths of inner experience.

As we will see in what follows, Mystical Christianity developed in many different forms and contexts. The forms range from those that experience God as an external reality who comes into, possesses, and takes over personal life, to those that experience the sacred as the depth and reality of one's own subjective life and experience. Whereas the former stresses the importance of self-sacrifice and the destruction of one's own will, feelings, and desires as a precondition of mystical union, the latter places more emphasis on self realization and on mysticism as the fulfilment and divinization of the unique individual in the Spirit of God. As for context, we will note the three main options for Mystical Christianity: to remain outside Church and Biblical Christianity (but face antagonism); to shelter within them (but face being controlled by power from on high); or to take shape in monastic contexts (under the umbrella of Church Christianity, but with considerable independence).

The beginnings of Christian mysticism and monasticism

Mysticism is not unique to Christianity, but Christianity supplied it with some distinctive ingredients. Jesus himself may exemplify a tendency towards a mystical 'internalization' of the Jewish religion, and the tendency could claim some scriptural backing. In the Book of Jeremiah in the Old Testament, for example, God speaks of the 'new covenant' he will establish with Israel:

> I will put my law within them, and I will write it upon their hearts . . . and no longer shall each man teach his neighbour . . . for they shall all know me, from the least of them to the greatest.

Far from being bound by the externals of the Law, Jesus takes it upon himself to interpret and even revise its teachings, claiming that it exists to serve humanity rather than vice versa, and criticizing those who use the Law to 'bind' their fellow humans. He is even more critical of the Jewish Temple and its cult, and, although his meaning is hard to reconstruct, he seems to have suggested that his own life – perhaps human life in general – is more important than a temple made of stones. He may mean something similar when he says: 'the sabbath was made for man, not man for the sabbath'.

Paul also displays some mystical tendencies, though his mysticism is best described as a 'Christ-mysticism'. 'It is no longer I who live', he says, 'but Christ who lives in me.' In his more radical moments, Paul believes that all baptized Christians are filled with the Spirit of Christ. In his more cautious moments, he counteracts the egalitarian potential of mysticism – that all may claim Christ-like authority – by using images of hierarchy to limit such claims. Christ, he says, is the 'head' of the church which is his 'body', and some Christians stand in closer relation to the head than others. So the Letter to the Ephesians (inspired by the Pauline tradition if not actually written by Paul) cautions: 'Wives, be subject to your husbands, as to the Lord. For the husband is the head of the wife as Christ is the head of the church.' Despite such precautions, however, Paul's theology had the potential to be appropriated by some of the more mystical forms of Christianity that competed with Church Christianity in the early centuries, as it was by the 'heretical' but highly successful Church of Marcion in the 2nd century. As a consequence, it took some time for Paul's letters to be accepted into the official canon of New Testament scripture.

Mystical currents were also present in Graeco-Roman culture: in some of the so-called 'mystery cults', in Persian and Far Eastern influences, and in the tradition of religio-philosophical thought flowing from Plato. The latter postulated a higher and more real spiritual world above the ephemeral material world and imagined the soul floating free of the body in order to ascend to the world of immaterial ideas. Some or all of these influences came together with the inspiration provided by Jesus in the 1st and 2nd centuries to produce the many different sorts of religious, spiritual, and philosophical groups and teachings that were lumped together by their opponents as 'gnostic'. So relentless was Church Christianity's attack that we know of gnosticism chiefly by way of 'orthodox' works of criticism by writers such as Irenaeus of Lyons (c. 130–c. 200) and Hippolytus (c. 170–236). It is only recently that some of the actual writings of these groups have been recovered. Contrary to the impression given by traditional church history, it is clear that these alternative interpretations of Christianity – and the groups with which they may have been associated – posed a serious threat to Church Christianity right up to the 4th century and beyond.

Discovery of gnostic scriptures has also undermined conventional summaries of gnosticism as involving: a secret knowledge ('gnosis'); a dualism that opposes an evil material world to a higher spiritual realm; a complicated cosmological myth of origins; belief in a divine redeemer figure who descends from the heavens; and a tendency towards renunciation of the world and the body. Some gnostic writings contain some of these elements, but by no means all. The writings associated with Valentinian and Sethian forms of gnosticism, for example, develop detailed cosmologies, whilst other works, such as the Gospel of Thomas, have no cosmological interest at all. Though it is hard to be clear about the nature of the groups that produced these scriptures, we can imagine a similar variety. Some may have taken the form of organized and centralized 'churches', whilst others would have been more reminiscent of the schools of philosophy that were still common in the Graeco-Roman world. Rather than having authoritative scriptures, rituals, or sacraments, members of such schools – often female as well as male – would be encouraged to think for themselves and debate with one another. In the Gospel of Thomas, for example, Jesus endorses the authority of women, rejects attempts to turn him into a figure of unique authority, instructs people that the truth is already within and around them, and encourages a view of the spiritual quest as an individual rather than a group enterprise (see Chapter 1).

Whereas Church Christianity embraced society and tried to win influence over it by allying itself with political power, the mystical tendency within early Christianity tended to be far more critical of both the church and the world. One reason was that it emphasized the 'things of the spirit' rather than the things of the world, and tended to view the externals of life – rituals, sacraments, material possessions, social status – as insignificant at best and dangerously distracting at worst. Another was that the belief that God empowers and divinizes all people who open themselves to His Spirit is naturally hostile to institutionalized hierarchies in church or society. The alliance between church and empire from the 4th century served only to reinforce some mystical Christians' suspicion that Church Christianity had departed from the pure spiritual path and betrayed the message of Jesus.

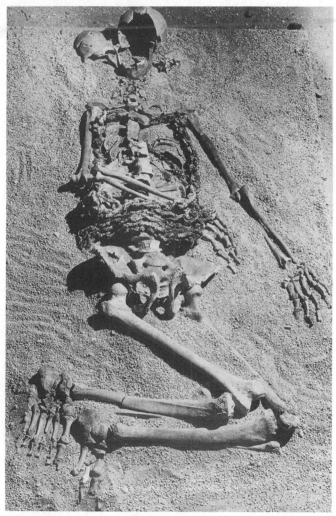

16. The skeleton of a young man bound in chains, found in a cave south of Jerusalem, near to an early Christian monastic settlement (Byzantine period). Chains were used for self-mortification, in order to 'conquer' the flesh and its desires. See overleaf.

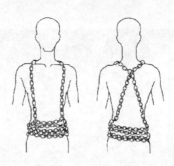

An increasingly common response on the part of those who wished to pursue spiritual perfection without distraction was literally to walk out on society in order to enter an uninhabited, unsocialized place – the desert. We first hear of men, and some women, journeying into the desert in significant numbers at the end of the 3rd century and the beginning of the 4th. Though they shared an ascetic desire to conquer the body and its passions in order to focus single-mindedly on the things of the spirit, they were probably diverse in other ways. Some wished to live the spiritual life in isolation, whilst others joined growing communities of spiritual seekers. In terms of later categories, some may have been 'gnostic', some more 'orthodox', and the majority probably a more complex mixture. Some helped lay the foundations of Christian monasticism.

We know of some early 'desert fathers' because their sayings have been preserved and collected together as the 'Sayings of the Desert Fathers'. These were men, and a few women, who ventured into the Egyptian desert and lived in solitude. But they consulted with more experienced 'abbas' (fathers), and shared their wisdom. Many had an ambitious aim: to attain the state of perfection that had been lost by Adam and Eve at the Fall and restored by Jesus. They sought to turn themselves into 'spiritual bodies', just as Christ had at his transfiguration and resurrection. In this state of perfection, human spirit would be united with God's Spirit, mind and senses calmed so that perception is clear and sharp, and the body returned to a state of such perfect equilibrium that it is able to survive beyond its

> # Extracts from *The Sayings of the Desert Fathers*
>
> The abbot Allois said, 'Unless a man shall say in his heart, "I alone and God are in this world", he shall not find quiet. He said again, "If a man willed it, in one day up till evening he might come to the measure of divinity".'
>
> There came to the abbot Joseph the abbot Lot, and said to him, 'Father, according to my strength I keep a modest rule of prayer and fasting and meditation and quiet, and according to my strength I purge my imagination: what more must I do?' The old man, rising, held up his hands against the sky, and his fingers became like ten torches of fire, and he said, 'If thou wilt, thou shalt be made wholly a flame'.

natural span with hardly any food or sleep. Far from exalting the achievements of the lonely hero of the faith, however, the desert fathers continually teach the importance of love, humility, and a sense of humour. Only by humbling himself or herself can a Christian hope to come close to the perfection of the God-man.

Mysticism and monasticism in the East

Mystical Christianity posed a threat to Church Christianity in many ways. It had scant regard for the externals of religion, including scripture and the sacraments, and it wished to claim for all Christians what Church Christianity reserved for Christ alone: divine-human status. As the fame of the desert ascetics increased, it threatened to undermine the claims of church and clergy. The ascetics were often compared to the martyrs, men and women prepared to witness to Christ through their suffering, and to leave the world rather than make compromises with it. Such spiritual heroism might make an uncomfortable contrast with a church that was busy making alliance with the very empire that was responsible for creating the martyrs through its persecutions in the first place.

The solution that gradually presented itself was for Church Christianity to co-opt the monastic movement and bring it under its own control. A key move was made by Athanasius who, in one of his many periods of enforced exile, spent time with the desert fathers. Athanasius harnessed the energy and prestige of monasticism for the developing Catholic Church in two ways. First, by ordaining ascetics and offering them places of responsibility and reward in the church, as well as by establishing orders of female virgins under the control of bishops. Second, by writing a highly influential *Life of Anthony* that celebrated one of the most revered desert fathers and presented him as a stalwart champion of the very brand of anti-Arian orthodoxy that Athanasius was himself defending, namely the orthodoxy ratified by the Council of Nicaea (see the previous chapter).

The consequences of this co-option of asceticism by the church were profound for both parties. As it began to come under the church's control, the mystical tendency in Christianity lost some of its freedom of manoeuvre. It became identified with the defence of 'orthodoxy' rather than with experimentation in the spiritual life, and with power from on high rather than power from below. In both West and East, the line dividing clergy from monks became blurred as higher clergy were increasingly drawn from monastic ranks. The church began to model its liturgy on monastic practice, whilst monasticism adopted the scriptural, sacramental, and sacerdotal bias of the church.

But the mystical impulse – and its more radical tendencies – did not wholly disappear, and in some circumstances monasticism was able to offer a congenial context, especially in the East. Here, to a much greater extent than in the West, monasteries retained considerable

> ## Extract from *The Revelations of St Seraphim of Sarov* (1759–1833)
>
> A dialogue between Seraphim and a seeker:
>
> > 'I don't understand how one can be certain of being in the spirit of God. How should I be able to recognize for certain this manifestation in myself?' . . .
> >
> > 'My friend, we are both at this moment in the Spirit of God . . . Why won't you look at me?'
> >
> > 'I can't look at you . . . Your eyes shine like lightening; your face has become more dazzling than the sun, and it hurts my eyes to look at you.'
> >
> > 'Don't be afraid', he said, 'at this very moment you've become as bright as I have. You also are present in the fullness of the Spirit of God; otherwise, you wouldn't be able to see me as you do see me.'

independence and were never organized into 'orders' under centralized clerical control. What is more, the eremetical tradition (the tradition of the hermit seeking communion with God in solitude) continued to exercise far more influence in the East than the West. Here, where Augustine's pessimistic view of human nature did not hold sway, the ideal of *theosis*, 'deification' or 'divinization' through the Holy Spirit, continued to be presented as the goal of the Christian life right through to the modern period. Whereas the West tended to venerate saints only after they were dead and buried, in the East the tradition of the living mystic and holy man continued unbroken from the days of the desert fathers (see Chapter 6).

Even in the East, however, there was a tendency for the individualistic inclinations of mysticism to be curbed and brought under the sway of Church Christianity – at least in the theological tradition. The greatest mystical theologians, notably Maximus the Confessor (580–662), Simeon the New Theologian (949–1022), and Gregory Palamas (1296–1359), refused to separate mysticism from full participation in the church's liturgy and sacraments. Their underlying argument was that the individual should not seek to be caught up in a mystical union of 'the alone with the Alone', but should seek God where the church indicates that He can be found – in the 'body of Christ' made present in icons, sacraments, and the worshipping community. In this vision the Church and Mystical types of Christianity reinforce and strengthen one another, rather than pulling apart.

Mysticism and monasticism in the West

In the West mysticism was more thoroughly assimilated to the programme of Church Christianity throughout the medieval period. A key step was the widespread adoption of Benedict's Rule (c. 540) as a charter for the organization of the monastic life. This Rule gave unity to monasticism as it spread across Europe and shaped it according to a common framework. Rather than providing space for individual contemplation and experience of the divine, the chief aim of Benedictine monasticism was to discipline monks so thoroughly that there was no room for the exercise of individual will or the development of a unique personal spirituality. Benedict envisaged the monastic life as one of obedience, silence, stability, renunciation of desire, and rigorous discipline. Most of a monk's time was taken up with the constant round of monastic offices – the eight worship services that punctuated the day – and the rest of the time with work. The theology of Augustine, whom Benedict greatly admired, and the development of Western monasticism, went hand in hand. By suppressing his own corrupted will, the monk could be brought into conformity with the will of God mediated by the abbot, the monastery, the Rule, and the church.

Extract from the Rule of St Benedict

In all things let all follow the Rule as their guide: and let no one diverge from it without good reason. Let no one in the monastery follow his own inclinations, and let no one boldly presume to dispute with the abbot . . . If anyone so presume, let him be subject to the discipline of the Rule. The abbot, for his part, should do everything in the fear of the Lord and in observance of the Rule; knowing he will surely have to give account to God for all his decisions.

The 11th and 12th centuries saw a new burst of enthusiasm for the monastic life in the west, and with it the beginnings of a revival of mysticism. A reform of Benedictine monasticism in the 10th century was succeeded by the foundation of many new orders. Some, like the highly successful Cistercian order, were designed to return to the severe asceticism from which it was felt that existing monasteries had strayed. Others, like the Carthusians, shared this ideal but revived aspects of the eremetical tradition. Women as well as men were caught up in the new enthusiasm for monasticism, often against the wishes of monastic leaders. Though it had been taking shape for several centuries, it was in this period that the Western monastic complex achieved its characteristic architectural form, with a church at its heart, accommodation on its south side, and a cloister connecting its various parts (see Fig. 17).

The controlled, ordered, and cloistered life of the monastery was unable, however, to contain the spiritual impulses of the medieval period. By the 13th century large numbers of devout Christian men and women sought an alternative context in which to live dedicated Christian lives. The very solidity and stability that had once commended monasticism now seemed to weigh it down. The fact

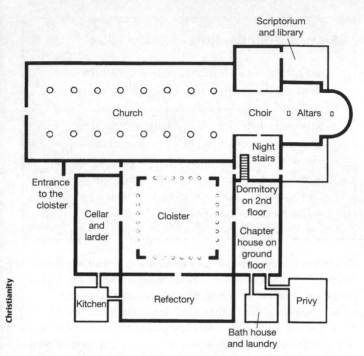

17. The plan of a medieval monastery with cloister, adapted from the Plan of St Gall, the earliest surviving architectural plan of the Middle Ages (c. 820).

that the monastery secured itself against the world counted against it in the eyes of those who wished to take the gospel into that world. As towns and cities grew, and with them new and very visible juxtapositions of wealth and poverty, the monastery was becoming less relevant to Europe's most pressing social and spiritual needs.

As we noted in the previous chapter, both the problem and the response were articulated in terms of a new ideal: the *via apostolica* (apostolic life). Its model was the life of Jesus and his followers: constantly on the move, bearing no money or possessions, carrying the gospel to all members of society. Inspired by this ideal, some

Christians simply took to the road on their own initiative – to the growing concern of the church authorities. Since they had no formal authorization from Rome, a good number of these wandering ascetics – such as the Waldenses – ended up being branded heretical. Others were more careful to seek Rome's approval. Once again, the church was astute enough to see the advantages of taking this new spiritual initiative under its wing.

The most important outcome was the legitimation of the new urban-based, mobile mendicant orders, first the Augustinian canons, then the Franciscan and Dominican friars, and much later the Jesuit order (Society of Jesus, founded by Ignatius of Loyola in 1540). Though many women shared the apostolic impulse, their options were more limited, for it was not thought suitable for them to be independent or mobile, or to preach. They were left with three main options: to remain within the home, to join a nunnery, or to enter into one of the growing number of communities of women who remained loyal to the church, but did not belong to a recognized order (the latter became known as 'beguines', and were formally condemned by the Council of Vienne in 1311–13, but survived for some time after this).

Although the revived monastic orders and the new mendicant orders gave some fresh impetus to mysticism in the medieval period, it tended to be those marginal to, or within, these institutions who made the most notable contribution. Many were women. Some of the most prominent, such as Hildegaard of Bingen (1098–1179), belonged to women's religious orders and received their education within them. Others, like Julian of Norwich (c. 1342–c. 1416) were hermits, and still others, for example Mechtild of Magdeburg (c. 1207–82) and Hadewijch (13th century), were beguines. A handful, like Teresa of Avila (1515–82), founded or reformed monastic orders in the face of considerable opposition from the church.

Whilst remaining loyal to Church Christianity, particularly its

Extract from Mechtild's *The Flowing Light of the Godhead*

God Rejoices that the soul has overcome four sins
Our Lord delights in Heaven
Because of the loving soul He has on earth,
And says, 'Look how she who has wounded Me has risen!
She has cast from her the apes of worldliness;
Overcome the bear of impurity,
Trodden the lion of pride underfoot,
Torn the wolf of desire from his revenge,
And comes racing like a hunted deer
To the spring which is Myself.
She comes soaring like an eagle
Swinging herself from the depths
Up into the heights.'

sacramental emphasis, women mystics sought a closer, more personal experience of the living God. They found it in a variety of subjective states: in intense experiences of communion with Jesus, in transports of delight, in experiences of inner suffering, abandonment, and darkness, and in union with the divine. Some, like Mechtild, used the sacraments as a point of direct contact with Jesus and positioned themselves as brides receiving the heavenly bridegroom. Others, like Teresa, favoured a form of contemplation that moved beyond images altogether and in which the self merged with the divine in an experience that could never be described. It was also possible to use mystical experiences as the basis for profound theological exploration, as when Julian developed a trinitarian theology on the basis of the 'showings' that God had vouchsafed to her many years before. To this rich variety was added the work of male mystical writers, many of whom were in close contact with women mystics and their communities, sometimes as spiritual advisers. They include Meister Eckhart (1260–1328), Johannes Tauler (1300–61), Jan van Ruysbroeck (1293–1381), and Gerhard Groote (1340–84). They too tended to exist on the fringes of the monastic and ecclesiastical establishment.

The medieval church's attitude was ambivalent. On the one hand, it could hardly deny the Godly hope that 'your sons and daughters will prophesy, your old men will dream dreams and your young men will see visions', for the Bible itself spoke of such things. On the other hand, Church Christianity viewed claims to unmediated contact with God with suspicion, and condemned any suggestion that the mystic could enter into union with God. Some of Eckhart's propositions were condemned on these grounds, and the beguine Marguerite Porete, author of the *Mirror of Simple Souls*, was burnt at the stake in 1310. Inquisitors were quick to accuse mystics of belonging to organized heretical movements of spiritual enthusiasm, such as the Brethren of the Free Spirit. Before long accusations of witchcraft would also begin to be levelled at women – and some men – who were believed to be grasping hold of the sacred in order to further their own, malevolent designs. In reality, however, there is little evidence that either mysticism or magic ever took shape in large-scale organized movements – other than in the imagination of the heresy-hunters themselves.

Mysticism in early Protestantism

Far from being confined to the Catholic Church, the mystical tendency in the West was also important in early Protestantism. In the 12th century Joachim of Fiore (c. 1135–1202) had foretold an Age of the Spirit in which *viri spiritualis* ('spiritual men') would inaugurate an era of love, freedom, and peace. Such hopes had intensified in the intervening centuries, and some saw in Luther the fulfilment of Joachim's prophecies. They had reasonable grounds for doing so. Not only had the young Luther been influenced by the German mystical tradition, but his early protests against the Catholic Church seemed to indicate his desire to abolish a religion of externals in order to replace it with a more inward-looking and spiritual form of Christianity. After all, it was Luther who argued that the inner conviction of grace in the heart of the believer was more important than external works, and Luther who announced the 'priesthood of all believers'.

Such hopes were dashed, however, when Luther and Calvin actually came to power. Far from leading the churches that took their name in a mystical direction, they retained the defining features of Church Christianity. Even Ulrich Zwingli (1484–1531), who had seemed to go furthest in the direction of a fully spiritual Christianity, pulled back from the full implications of his position. Supporters of the Reformation who had hoped for a different outcome were forced to create their own, more radical forms of Protestantism. Some of these took a Biblical form (see the previous chapter), whilst others located authority in the Spirit more than the Word. Of the latter, the most notorious were those experiments that tried to bring about dramatic social change here and now, often in the 'apocalyptic' expectation that this would precipitate God's rule on earth. Thomas Müntzer (c. 1489–1525) became a leader of the German peasants' rebellion of 1525, and the town of Münster became a centre of apocalyptic expectation and social experimentation. Both initiatives were crushed by the combined forces of church and state, with both Catholic and Protestant Church Christianity united in their violent opposition to such mystically inspired political upheaval.

Though 'Müntzer and Münster' became a byword for the dangers inherent in Mystical Christianity, apocalyptic activism was the exception rather than the norm. The mystical tendency in Protestantism gave rise to many different versions of Christian community, few of which engaged in direct political action, but some of which constituted at least an implicit threat to the existing forms of higher power. Luther's disillusioned colleague Andreas

Rudolf Bodenstein von Karlstadt (c. 1480–1541), for example, rejected the idea of a state-supported church of external authority in favour of voluntary, egalitarian groups of lay people led by spiritually enlightened souls elected by the whole congregation. Others, like Kaspar von Schwenkfeld (1489–1561) and Sebastian Franck (c. 1499–c. 1542), had no interest in establishing new churches, but thought that spiritual seekers should form their own small groups for mutual edification and support. The latter idea helped inspire Pietism, a reforming movement within the Lutheran churches that became widely influential in Prussia in the late 17th and early 18th centuries, and whose political quietism and charitable activism eventually won it state support. Pietism, in turn, had a direct influence on John Wesley (1703–91) and his brother Charles (1707–88), the founders of Methodism.

The only mystical group that succeeded in founding an independent, unified, lasting, and influential community of its own was the Society of Friends, or Quakers. Its founder George Fox (1624–91) rejected existing forms of Christianity in his quest for a pure, inward, spiritual religion based on direct experience of Christ in the heart of the individual. Fox spoke of the light of Christ that illuminates each individual directly, and believed that those who know the indwelling presence of Christ have no need of external channels of grace. He therefore removed all sacraments, ritual, liturgy, priests, and scriptures from worship. Friends gather not in 'churches' but in 'meeting houses', and in worship they sit together in silence unless and until someone is moved by the Spirit to speak. In practice, however, Quakerism survived by combining a pure and formless mysticism with a Biblical and Christological basis and a sophisticated organizational form.

Conclusion

Rather than being allowed to float free, establish its own institutions, or become the prerogative of individuals unattached to any form of sacred association, Christian mysticism was rarely able to escape the influence of Church Christianity – and later, Biblical Christianity – altogether. Monasticism served as a sort of intermediate institution in which some individuals were able to dedicate themselves to the mystical path, without departing too radically from the teaching and control of the church and clergy.

This is almost certainly one reason why most varieties of Christian mysticism in the pre-modern period do not go to the extreme pole of the Christian spectrum in which the sacred is located wholly within individual experience and selfhood – even to the extent of being identified with it – rather than being set over against it. Although some of the earliest forms of Christian mysticism tended in this direction, they were quickly styled 'gnostic' and 'heretical' and banished from the mainstream of Christian life. Later mystics who were suspected of moving too far in this direction were subject to official condemnation by the church.

This probably explains why, when the early modern period witnessed the rise of a style of mysticism that fused Christian and Romantic influences (as in the writings of William Blake (1757–1827) in England, or the Transcendentalists in America), it was usually regarded as having placed itself beyond the limits of what counted as Christian. What sets such Romantic mysticism apart from most other varieties of Christian mysticism is its sense that God is to be found *within* the deepest desires, experiences, and sensations of human life – including those associated with sex. By contrast, most of the mysticism reviewed above maintains that individuals have to destroy their personal desires, experiences, aptitudes, and distinctiveness in order that God can enter into their lives and take control of it. Thus the divine remains in some significant way external to human nature and opposed to it. In most Christian mysticism God is the king, bridegroom, and lover to whom the soul must surrender, submit, and sacrifice itself before He can 'enter in' and take possession.

Chapter 5

Modern Christianity: the West

Having considered the unfolding of Christianity in its several varieties, we are now in a position to consider its interactions with modernity. For Christianity there have really been *two* modernities. In cultural terms, the first was inaugurated by the Enlightenment of the 18th century, which gave new authority to human reason and the freedom to exercise it. Socio-economically it was characterized by the rise of urban-industrial society and politically by the rise of nation states governed by increasingly powerful centralized governments. The second (or 'late') modernity began much later, in the 1960s, and one of its defining cultural characteristics is a turn to subjective-life, which involves a flight from deference – to any established external authority, religious or secular – and an embrace of the authority of one's own deepest feelings, intuitions, desires, and experiences. The turn to subjective-life is reinforced by other developments, including the triumph of democracy in the political sphere and capitalism in the economic sphere (accompanied by growing affluence). Together these changes conspire to give the unique individual self and its choices new weight and significance.

What this chapter will show is that whereas Christianity was eventually relatively successful in adapting to the first modernity, it has found the second far less congenial. It will also reveal, however, that some varieties of Christianity have coped with the subjective turn somewhat better than others.

'Enlightened' reaction against Christianity

As we saw in Chapter 3, the dominant form of Christianity – Church Christianity – entered the modern period in close alliance with the emerging nation states of Europe. Each nation had its state church, whether Catholic or Protestant (indeed a whole denomination – the Church of England or 'Anglican Church' – come into being, in part, to discharge this role). Alliance between church and state in the early modern world was strengthened by a shared worldview. State churches endorsed the view that power was the proper possession of a monarch – God in the heavens, the king on earth – who had the right and duty to command his people. The people, in turn, were obliged to obey sovereign power from on high in both its earthly and heavenly manifestations.

Whereas Christianity in pre-Reformation Europe had served as a focus of unity, with a single church – the Roman Catholic – transcending the rivalries of secular powers, Christianity now became a factor *in* such rivalry. Growing antagonism and warfare between competing nation states became bound up with rivalries between Catholic and Protestant, not to mention those between different varieties of Protestantism. In the process, Christianity became more 'confessional' than before, with competing churches articulating what they stood for – and what set them apart – by way of propositional statements of faith ('confessions'). Christianity also became more evangelistic, as different denominations grew more competitive and more concerned to win converts to their own particular version of the truth. Far from acting as an agent of peace and unity, Christianity seemed to be exacerbating the intolerance, hostility, and warfare that had become such a characteristic feature of early modern Europe.

In the wake of the violent upheavals of the English Civil War and the wars of religion that raged across Continental Europe in the 17th century, some English and French writers began to propose radical reform. The so-called 'Deists' made trenchant criticisms of 'traditional' Christianity, accusing it of being both irrational and intolerant. Rather than advocating atheism, however, they proposed a new rational 'natural' religion that would offer a firmer basis for a stable and prosperous society. Based on reason rather than superstition, such religion would abandon belief in such things as miracles, the virgin birth, and the Trinity, and would retain only the more rational and ethical elements of Christianity: belief in a creator God, in the brotherhood of man, the immortality of the soul, and the duty of love and care for one another.

Deism represents the first modern manifestation of a 'Liberal' form of Christianity, that is to say a Christianity that accepts the authority of human reason, the value of freedom, and the possibility of progress. Liberal Christianity takes a relatively high view of human dignity (closer to Aquinas than Augustine), but believes that it is cultivated by way of belief in the Christian God, and in the context of the church. As we will see in the remainder of this chapter, Liberal Christianity played an important role in the rise of first modernity, and did far more than merely accommodate itself passively to modern values. It always faced the danger, however, of being viewed as an uneasy compromise between a more wholehearted embrace of human reason, freedom, and dignity, on the one hand, or a more devout and humble submission to the mysteries of the Christian faith and the authority of God and His church, on the other.

The most dramatic historical clash between these two extremes – the extremes that Liberal Christianity tried to move between – occurred in the French Revolution of 1789. The Roman Catholic Church in France had become closely bound up with the monarchy, and legitimated the latter's increasingly despotic rule as the will of God. By the 18th century currents of Enlightened thought were gathering force in Europe, with pockets of intense support in France, and the enthusiastic embrace of human dignity, liberty, and equality was leading to growing criticism of the religious as well as the political establishment. Though it was dangerous to voice atheistic sentiment explicitly, philosophers like Voltaire (1694–1778) came close to developing what amounted to a fully secular position, in which man relies on his own abilities and abandons all tutelage to God.

Political and intellectual protest went hand in hand in France. Given the close alliance between church and state, rebellion against the monarchy almost inevitably involved rebellion against the Catholic Church as well. When eventually the Revolution got underway – given the opportunity by an economic crisis – it did so under the banner of 'freedom, equality, and brotherhood'. The privileges of power on high supported by Church Christianity for so long were challenged by new aspirations towards democracy. Belief that power was the God-given privilege of the few was challenged by the belief that it was the natural possession of all the people (or at least all property-owning males). Although some revolutionaries drew the conclusion that the overthrow of tyranny must include the overthrow of the church, in the event a more moderate and pragmatic policy of 'secularization' was pursued in France, one that aimed not to abolish the church but to bring it under greater public control.

The Roman Catholic Church responded with vigour. It condemned the French Revolution and the ideals that inspired it, including the desire for freedom and the aspiration towards democracy. It reasserted its monarchial ideals, and continued in its work of centralizing the church and extending its control over personal life and, where possible, political life as well. It condemned new currents of thought, and encouraged the production of 'manuals' of confessional Catholic theology based on the work of Aquinas. The papacy defended its position as an important powerbroker within Europe, and wherever and whenever the cause of democracy stalled, it was poised and ready to take advantage. As late as 1864, the Catholic Church issued a condemnation of the errors of modern

Extracts from *The Syllabus of Errors*

[Errors condemned by the Pope:]

15. Every man is free to embrace and profess that religion which, guided by the light of reason, he shall consider true . . .

24. The church has not the power of using force, nor has she any temporal power, direct or indirect . . .

44. The civil authority may interfere in matters relating to religion, morality and spiritual government . . .

77. In the present day it is no longer expedient that the Catholic religion should be held as the only religion of the State, to the exclusion of all other forms of worship . . .

80. The Roman Pontiff can, and ought to, reconcile himself, and come to terms with progress, liberalism and modern civilization.

reason, progress, and democracy – *The Syllabus of Errors* – and in 1870 it propounded the Doctrine of Papal Infallibility. In the process Roman Catholicism became more closely identified with the forces of social conservatism than democracy and social change.

The democratization of Christianity

Not all the Christian churches reacted against revolutionary and democratic upheavals in the same way as the Roman Catholic Church in Europe. In 1776 another revolution had taken place, against British colonial rule in what would become the United States of America. There were close links between the American and French revolutions, and many shared ideals. But whereas the revolution in France put Christianity on the defensive, the outcome in America was rather different. Even though Britain had exported its state church, the Anglican Church, it had allowed other churches to establish themselves in American territory. Rather than ally themselves *against* the forces of revolution, many of these churches supported the cause of independence and freedom.

It would be an exaggeration to say that Christianity generated the democratic constitution of the United States. The men who laid the political foundations of the newly independent nation were mainly Deists who supported various forms of post-confessional rational religion. But there were many rather more traditional Church and Biblical Christians in America who were genuinely supportive of the Revolution and its ideals and who believed that good Christians could also be good Americans, loyal to the ideals of liberty and democracy.

One explanation of the greater openness towards the modern secular, democratic state on the part of many American churches is that they had more to gain than to lose from constitutional separation of church and state. Since there were already many competing confessions in the USA, they had no desire to see one of their number elevated to the position of a state church. Some already had direct experience of being a minority faith in Europe, and had fled to the USA in order to escape the disadvantages and persecutions that could attend such status. Some of the churches that fell into this category were of the Church type (Congregationalists, Presbyterians), others Biblical (Baptists), some between the two (Methodists), and some more Mystical in orientation (Quakers). Although Congregationalist, Presbyterian, and Catholic churches had no ideological preference for church—state separation and religious toleration, they accommodated these ideals for pragmatic reasons, and before long their pragmatic preference was being justified in terms of theological commitment (resulting in stormy relations between the Catholic Church in America and that in Rome). The Biblical and Mystical churches were in a stronger ideological position to support democratic freedoms, given their long history of opposition to political and religious hierarchy and their support for more democratic arrangements in their own institutional life.

The upshot was that the rise of the secular nation state and the gradual extension of democratic arrangements did less damage to Christianity in America than in Europe. One could even argue that the churches profited, in so far as they presented themselves as foundational to 'the American way'. We can see the results to this day in the fact that levels of churchgoing in the USA are about twice as high as those in Europe, and religion continues to play a more central role in the culture and even in political life (albeit informally). Paradoxically, the formal separation of church and state allowed far more mutual support of the one by the other in the USA than did continuing establishment in much of Europe.

The 19th century

The 19th century is sometimes presented as the most intensely Christian era the West has ever known, and sometimes as the point at which secularism first began to challenge Christian cultural hegemony in a serious way. There is truth in both accounts.

On the one hand, the 19th century witnessed a massive explosion in the numbers of churches, clergy, and churchgoers, to a greater extent than can be accounted for by population growth. Many of the ecclesiastical buildings that still have a prominent place in the built environment came into existence at this time, and many of the institutions and practices we still associate with Christianity were invented or came into their own, including Sunday schools, Bible classes, Bibles and prayer books that ordinary people could afford to own, Sunday Communion services, Gothic Revival furnishing and architecture, and popular pictures and sculptures of Jesus and the saints. Amongst believers piety rose to a new pitch of intensity and commitment. In Britain, for example, up to half the population attended church on an average Sunday, some attending more than once. Christian literature – books, magazines, and novels – reached a peak of production, and Christian language and values permeated the general culture. Thrift, hard work, temperance, self-reliance, cleanliness, respectability, family values, sexual continence – it was hard to say whether these were general cultural values or Christian values, so closely intertwined had the two become (see Fig. 18).

On the other hand, doubt and disillusionment with Christianity became perhaps more prevalent, and certainly more public, than ever before. It was fuelled, in part, by the growing prestige of scientific method. The tangible success of science in explaining the world and giving rise to technological innovation was hard to argue with. Since science worked on an empirical basis, seeking knowledge by way of patient exploration of the world around rather than by reference to supernatural revelation, it seemed to undermine the confessional theological method of deduction from first principles believed to have been revealed directly by God. This impression was reinforced when science made discoveries, or proposed theories, that directly contradicted the Bible and theology. One of the earliest was geology's discovery that the earth was far, far older than the 6,006 years that some theologians had calculated on the basis of the Biblical record. The application of critical historical methods to the Bible further unsettled faith by placing question marks over hitherto secure beliefs (that Moses had written the first five books of the Bible, that the gospels contained the authentic words of Jesus, and so on). Darwin caused further unrest by contradicting the account of creation in Genesis and its anthropocentric view that the world had been created for the benefit of human beings. Most devastating of all was the fact that Darwin's theory of evolution offered the first plausible account of how life might have come into being as the result not of purposive design but blind chance.

18. *Family at Church*, by H. Fitzcook. Illustration from *The Sunday at Home* (1865).

Undaunted by such enormous challenges, Liberal Christianity faced and met them head on. Liberals rejected the idea that God's truth could simply be read out of the Bible and the writings of the church fathers and applied to the world in a deductive manner, and they believed that reason, free thought, and the scientific method could be made the friend, not the enemy, of Christian belief. After all, if

Friedrich Schleiermacher

Schleiermacher (1768–1834) is credited with setting the (Liberal) agenda for modern theology, an agenda that dominated academic theology until the later part of the 20th century. He also helped turn the tide against the deductive, propositional, dogmatic form of theology that had become characteristic of the confessional age. Schleiermacher understood why his contemporaries rejected a form of Christianity that seemed to have no real connection to life, but he argued that they had misunderstood the true nature of *The Christian Faith* (also the title of one of his most important works). Such faith, he argued, had more to do with a feeling of absolute dependence than with assent to a set of propositions. In saying this, Schleiermacher was in effect grounding Christianity on our deepest human experiences, though he insisted that such experiences are most fully and adequately interpreted by the scriptures and in the light of Christ.

God had made the world, there was nothing humans could discover about 'nature' that could undermine belief in its creator. Liberal Theology therefore granted science sovereignty in its own sphere: in telling us about the material world and its workings. But it reserved to itself the job of telling us what we could know about God and how we should behave in order to please Him. In the process, theology became more ethical in emphasis and more willing to acknowledge the value of human experience – especially moral experience – as a basis for our knowledge of God.

Liberal Theology's great achievement was to make it possible to be rational yet remain a Christian. Not only did it accept the validity of the scientific method in its own sphere, it even managed to assimilate Darwin by arguing that evolution was not an alternative to divine creation, but the method through which such creation took place. For Liberals, accounts like that of creation in Genesis were 'myths' that contain deep spiritual truths but should not be confused with scientific treatises.

Although they were able to make very significant intellectual concessions to a modern, rational sensibility, Liberal Christians tended to be more conservative when it came to the church and its role in society. Many Liberals were Church Christians who remained committed to the vision of a society guided by Christian values, and respectful of the church, its sacraments and clergy. Though it gave rise to some distinctively Liberal denominations, most notably the Unitarian Church, Liberalism was most influential within existing denominations, and it had a particular affinity with Protestant Church Christianity. Since the latter was very much in the ascendant in the 19th century – not least because it was the dominant tradition in the most powerful nations and empires of the day, including Britain and America – Liberal Christianity found itself in a position of great influence. It managed to support the interests and values of the newly powerful middle classes and their politicians, whilst at the same time maintaining a social conscience by calling for amelioration of the conditions of the industrial working classes.

But by no means all Christians were sympathetic to the Liberal programme. Liberal voices within the Catholic Church were silenced and suppressed, and the enterprise of Biblical criticism was banned. In the Protestant camp too, some were hostile to the liberalization of the faith and suspicious of the alliance between Liberal Christianity and middle-class interests. Biblical Christians were likely to be hostile on two counts: first, that the truths of the Bible were being compromised; and second, that the church and 'the world' were becoming too cosy by half. The assimilation of Darwin proved the final straw that broke the camel's back. By the turn of the century conservative Biblical Christians, in the USA in particular, were defending 'creationism' (the belief that God created the world in the way described in Genesis), and attacking Darwin and his Liberal Christian supporters. The movement came to public expression early in the 20th century as 'Fundamentalism', so-called because of its desire to return to the 'fundamentals' of Christian belief.

Christianity and the turn to subjective-life

Despite growing opposition, Liberal Christianity entered the 20th century in robust good health. Right up to the 1970s, it seemed reasonable to think that the powerful alliance of Liberal Theology, Church Christianity, and middle-class values would continue to dominate the Christian landscape in the West for the foreseeable future. Liberal theologians like Rudolph Bultmann (1884–1976) and Paul Tillich (1886–1965) helped set the intellectual agenda of Christianity, the 'liberal mainline' churches had been boosted by a widespread return to 'home and church' in the immediate aftermath of World War II, and even the Catholic Church seemed to be travelling in a liberal direction in the wake of the Second Vatican Council (1962–5). The latter, convened by Pope John XXIII, brought to an end a 'fortress' mentality that had seen the Roman Catholic Church turn its back on modern culture and retreat into a world of Thomistic scholarship, affective piety, and obedience to Rome. The Council opened the door to a number of important changes in Catholic life and thought, including the use of the vernacular rather than Latin in worship, the introduction of modern hymns and choruses, the liberalization of the religious life for Catholic monks and nuns, a more critical approach to Biblical and theological studies, and an acceptance of the principles of religious freedom and toleration. The Council also ratified a new self-understanding in which the church was identified with 'the whole people of God' rather than the clerical hierarchy.

By the end of the 20th century, however, Liberalism was in retreat. A brief increase in churchgoing after the Second World War had turned into precipitous decline, and Church Christianity was particularly badly affected. Between 1970 and 2000, regular Sunday attendance in the Anglican, Methodist, Roman Catholic, and United Reformed churches in England roughly halved, for example. Liberal mainline churches fared little better elsewhere in Europe, or even in North America. Many of the churches that suffered most were the old state churches. Sunday attendance in the Church of Sweden, for example, fell to below 2% of the population by the end of the century, whilst attendance in the Church of England halved in just two decades (between 1980 and 2000). Liberal Theology also suffered a reversal of fortunes. Having once dominated the theological stage, it now found itself on the defensive. New developments of a broadly liberal tendency, such as Feminist Theology and Liberation Theology (see the following chapters), served merely to make the Liberal agenda seem old-fashioned.

As Liberal Christian fortunes fell, so conservative ones rose. The Biblical churches fared particularly well. Even though Fundamentalism had been rubbished by the liberal establishment in America in the 1920s, conservative Christians in the USA managed to construct a successful Christian subculture with its own churches, schools, colleges, shops, radio and television channels, and networks of association. This culture managed to hold its own against the corrosive influences of popular culture, to increase its numbers, and to make its voice heard on the American political scene in the 1980s and even later. Its energies have been directed towards defending the 'traditional home', 'family values', and clearly differentiated roles for men and women. It has been particularly active in campaigns against homosexuality and abortion and in favour of sexual abstinence before marriage. In some instances conservative Catholics and Protestants have joined together in these campaigns.

The broader trajectory of 'Evangelical Christianity' has been even more successful. Though they do not take as extreme a stand as Fundamentalists on issues such as Biblical inerrancy, Evangelicals

Karl Barth

Liberal Theology came under fierce attack by the Swiss Reformed theologian Karl Barth (1886–1968). His first influential book was his *Commentary on Romans*, in which he stressed the unbridgeable distance that separates God and humanity. Barth accused Liberals of cutting God down to human size by trying to capture him in the categories of human understanding. In his later, multi-volume *Church Dogmatics*, Barth argued that humans can understand God only on the basis of God's own revelation in the Word (that is, in Christ, scripture, and faithful preaching). Against those who suggested that many religions contain truth, Barth argued that all religion is an idolatrous human construction that can never reach up to the living God. In order to 'let God be God', theologians must abandon their attempts to comprehend God, and have the humility to rely on God's Word alone. Barth helped revitalize Christian theology by asserting its unique relationship to truth, and by the later part of the 20th century the 'neo-orthodox' approach he inspired had become dominant in academic theology.

affirm the supreme authority of the Bible, the sinfulness of humanity, full and perfect salvation through the work of Jesus Christ on the cross, the necessity of giving one's life to Jesus and being 'born again', the importance of a strict Biblical morality that affirms family values, and active evangelization. With its roots in the early modern era, Evangelicalism grows out of a confessional context, but abandons intra-Protestant rivalries for cooperation. Whilst retaining a propositional approach to the Christian faith (faith as assent to lists of propositions), it combines this with a more modern emphasis on the importance of direct experience of the sacred (particularly in the experience of being 'born again' in the Spirit). Evangelicals may belong to any of the historic Protestant churches, or to independent congregations. They consider these divisions of 'churchmanship' less important than the experiences and affirmations that bind them together.

In its growing emphasis on the importance of individual experience, Evangelicalism has also been influenced by another pan-denominational movement, Charismatic Christianity (which embraces Pentecostalism, and may also be called Pentecostal Christianity). Charismatic Christianity, which will be examined in more detail in the next chapter, places particular emphasis upon the direct experience of God as Holy Spirit. As a result, Evangelical Protestantism now covers a spectrum of positions. At one extreme are the most conservative Evangelicals, or Fundamentalists, who affirm the absolute and infallible authority of scripture. At the other are Charismatic Evangelicals (or Evangelical Charismatics), who affirm the authority of scripture and of direct experience of the Holy Spirit. There are also some Charismatic Catholics whose Catholicism has been influenced by the experiential stress of the Charismatic movement.

Pulling all this together, we can present Christianity in the modern period as internally differentiated depending on where it locates ultimate authority: in God, in human reason enlightened by God, or in subjective experience more broadly (including not just reason but intuition and feelings). If we lay this scheme of categorization across the broader scheme used in the previous two chapters to classify historic Christianity (Church, Biblical, and Mystical types), we can represent the different varieties of modern Christianity by way of a simple diagram (see page 104).

This diagram also helps us understand the changing fortunes of Christianity in modern times. Since the transition to first modernity involved a cultural shift away from transcendent authority towards the authority of individual reason (from left to the centre on the

	Transcendent authority	*Rational authority*	*Experiential authority*
Church type	*Conservative Catholicism* *Conservative Anglicanism, Lutheranism, Presbyterianism*	*Liberal Catholicism* *Liberal Protestantism*	*Pentecostal Catholicism*
Biblical type	*Fundamentalism* *Evangelicalism*	*Liberal Evangelicalism*	*Charismatic/ Pentecostal Christianity*
Mystical type	*Mystical Eastern Orthodoxy*	*Swedenborgianism* *Christian Science*	*Society of Friends*

Varieties of Christianity in the modern world.

diagram), it favoured Liberal Christianity (or secular rationalism). Since the transition to second modernity involved disillusionment with scientific rationality and a growing turn to subjective-life, it favoured more experiential forms of religion and spirituality (moving to the right of the diagram). As this turn to subjective-life has become more widespread since the 1960s, so successive generations have become increasingly alienated from a Church Christianity (conservative or liberal) which offers little by way of subjective experience and tends to place more emphasis on religious and moral duty and social conformity than on the value of 'living my own life in my own way' (one might say they have dropped off the right-hand side of the diagram altogether).

Some conservative Biblical churches have also declined, particularly those that have failed to make room for individual experience. The form of Christianity that has fared best since the 1970s is that which falls into the category of 'Biblical-Experiential' in the diagram above, most notably the Charismatic and Evangelical Charismatic churches. The latter bring together the Biblical and Mystical varieties of Christianity. For those who are somewhat wary of the subjective turn, they offer clear Bible-based belief and moral authority, but manage to combine it with the promise of subjective experience, satisfaction, self-development, and well-being. Though the Father God may remain an external authority figure, Jesus Christ is experienced directly as an ever-present companion and guide, entering into life by way of the Spirit. The more Charismatic the church, the more that intense, ecstatic experiences of possession by the Holy Spirit will be emphasized (see the next chapter).

To some extent, as one would expect, the subjective turn of second modernity has also benefited the mystical tendency in Christianity. Traditional Church Christianity has occasionally been able to buck the trend of decline where it has been able to cater to the demand for personally meaningful mystical 'spirituality' by offering moving and inspiring worship services in beautiful historic settings. Some historic mystical churches have also fared well, including Quaker and Unitarian congregations that have moved in a subjectivized direction. The reason that Mystical Christianity has not done even better, given the growing cultural demand for spirituality that caters to subjective-life, is probably that it now faces so much competition from alternative spiritual providers. The closing decades of the 20th century witnessed the rapid growth of 'holistic' forms of spirituality, ranging from spiritual Yoga to Tai Chi to Reiki. With more and more people identifying themselves as 'spiritual' rather than 'religious', and with fewer and fewer having a Christian background, such holistic spirituality looks set to flourish

Overall, then, the late 20th century has not been kind to the Western churches. In many parts of Europe, regular Sunday attendance levels had declined to between 4 and 8% of the population by the turn of the millennium (with monthly attendance

19. This disused chapel in the north of England (above) has been sold by the United Reformed Church and is in the process of being converted into a Meditation Centre (below). The Meditation Centre is not affiliated to any particular faith, and caters to the growing numbers of Westerners interested in 'spirituality not religion'.

levels about one and a half times greater). Even in the USA, the best estimates put weekly Sunday churchgoing as low as 20% – though self-reported attendance is almost twice as high. Having already lost a good deal of political and economic power in the early modern period, Christianity now lost much of the cultural power it had managed to retain and even consolidate in the 19th century. Where once it had been part of the 'establishment', Christianity now became part of a conservative counter-culture, protesting against secular values and the subjective turn of modern culture and calling for a return to traditional values, community, and family. Some Liberal and Mystical Christians fought a rearguard action on behalf of wide social concern, sexual tolerance, and a greater openness to sacred power from within. But the mood of theology, of church leadership, and of popular Christian feeling had turned against them – even though the most successful forms of Christianity had made some significant concessions to the subjective turn.

Conclusion

The simplest way of presenting the story of Christianity in the modern West would be to say that a religion that had long favoured power from on high found itself in a context in which power from below – the power of each and every individual – was winning the day. Finding itself out of tune with the times, Christianity suffered a massive loss of support – both social and individual – and reacted by becoming more defensive and counter-cultural. As this chapter has demonstrated, however, such an analysis can be sharpened by paying more attention to the internal diversity of Christianity, and to the varied fortunes of the religion's different strands.

The dominant form of Christianity, Church Christianity, entered first modernity in a form that was likely to prove incompatible with the new emphasis being placed on human reason and dignity. Clashes were inevitable, and occurred most dramatically where a church refused to give any quarter to the new humanistic values – as in France. Elsewhere, however, Church Christianity managed to liberalize, and to become the ally rather than the enemy of modernization. A relatively harmonious relationship was established between church, society, and culture in the 19th century, not least because the church still had a role to play in upholding social hierarchy, particularly the interests of the new middle classes.

In the 20th century the fortunes of Church Christianity began to change as it was squeezed and criticized from two sides. On the one hand, more conservative Church and Biblical Christians began to criticize Liberal Christians for qualifying Christian truth. On the other hand, even such Liberalism proved unable to cater to the new demands being placed on the sacred by a culture that was increasingly focused on the cultivation and development of personal subjective-life. As a result, Liberal Church Christianity has suffered massive decline in recent decades; Mystical Christianity has fared somewhat better; but the most successful churches of all have been those that have managed to combine an emphasis on the authority of the Bible with the offer of personal, subjective empowerment through the Holy Spirit.

Chapter 6
Christianity beyond the West

At exactly the same time that Christianity went into serious decline in the West it entered a phase of rapid growth in the southern hemisphere. By the last quarter of the 20th century, Charismatic Christianity had become one of the fastest growing forms of religion in the world, second only to resurgent Islam. Like the latter, its success has tended to be greatest in areas that had formerly been under Western colonial control.

Before examining this latest phase in Christian history, this chapter takes a step backwards in time. Since its topic is Christianity beyond the West, it is important to remember that Christianity has never been a straightforwardly Western religion. The chapter begins, therefore, by looking at Christian expansion in the East and by bringing the history of Eastern Orthodoxy up to date. It then turns its attention to the global expansion of the Western churches after the 16th century, before returning to the topic of recent indigenous growth in Latin America, sub-Saharan Africa, and parts of Asia.

Eastern Christianity and its expansion

There are some good reasons for regarding early Christianity as an Eastern rather than a Western religion. It emerges from the religion and culture of a Semitic people. It spreads rapidly into the western part of Roman Empire, but its most important centres are in the Greek-speaking East, not the Latin-speaking West. This orientation to the East is consolidated by Constantine's transfer of the imperial capital from Rome to Constantinople and by the gradual transformation of the classical Roman Empire into the Christian Byzantine Empire (see Chapter 3).

Christianity's centre of gravity might have shifted even further east had Roman plans to conquer Persia come to fruition. But Christian communities had in any case established themselves in Persia and further afield even without Roman assistance. Their survival depended upon the rulers in whose territories they were located. In Persia Christianity flourished so long as it had the support of the ruling Sassanian dynasty. With important intellectual centres in Edessa and Nisibis, Persian Christianity developed its own distinctive theological emphases under the influence of theologians such as Theodore of Mopsuestia (c. 350–428) and Nestorius (mid-4th to mid-5th centuries). It was this tradition of thought that led eventually to the split, noted in Chapter 3, between the 'orthodox' Christology of the Byzantine Church and the 'Nestorian' Christology of the 'Church of the East' (also called the 'Nestorian Church'). Though based in Persia, Nestorian Christianity spread further east along the busy trade routes that connected the Roman and Persian empires with Asia. By about the 6th century, small Christian communities had been established as far afield as India and China, as well as in parts of Africa.

But the eastern extension of Christianity was inhibited by the existence of entrenched Confucian, Hindu, and Buddhist cultures that pre-dated Christianity and resisted its incursions. Without political backing Christianity was unable to do more than win over small, marginal social groups that had something to gain from conversion to a foreign religion not immediately associated with a dominant power. After the death of Muhammed in 632, Christian expansion was also inhibited by the growing power of Islam.

Though it drew on elements of both Jewish and Christian monotheism, this new faith proved far more successful in converting the Arabic speaking peoples of the Middle East, and was soon winning converts in North Africa and the Near East as well (the Persian Empire fell in the mid-7th century). Whereas Christianity had appealed mainly to city dwellers and had kept intact the Roman economic system based on slavery, Islam appealed to those in rural areas as well, and promised a more thoroughgoing reconstruction of society. By bringing together military, political, and religious power in a compact alliance, Islam brought to an end once and for all the long-cherished hope of a Christian world empire.

As a result of its failures to expand, 'orthodox' Byzantine Christianity became more entrenched around Constantinople. Still confident in its status as the religion of God's holy empire on earth, it set about consolidating its position. Church and emperor worked in the closest cooperation, their aim being to shape their earthly kingdom in conformity to its heavenly pattern. The public life of empire was scripted by way of elaborate rituals and ceremonies, and a rigid social hierarchy developed in imitation of the celestial hierarchy. It was within this context that the form of Church Christianity we now call 'Eastern Orthodoxy' or simply 'Orthodoxy' developed its distinctive identity. It viewed itself as the one true church of Christ and the apostles, and based its life and thought on the seven ecumenical councils of the church (from Nicaea I in 325 to Nicaea II in 787). Though the church in Rome and its pope began to make increasingly grandiose claims for themselves, Byzantium was never in any doubt that *it* was still the Holy Roman Empire and that the Pope had no authority over the Patriarch in Constantinople. When the West began to make liturgical and doctrinal innovations, including the addition of the 'filioque' to the creed (saying the Holy Spirit proceeds from 'the Father and the Son' rather than 'the Father' alone), Orthodoxy reacted with dismay. Such developments convinced it that its duty must be to guard the true faith against change and innovation.

20. The world of Eastern Orthodoxy.

This is not to imply that the Byzantine church lost its expansive
drive; if anything competition with the West encouraged it to seek
new converts. Though hemmed in by Islam on several sides, the
Orthodox Church was able to direct its expansive energies into
Romania and the Slavic lands of Bulgaria, Serbia, and Russia.
Despite competition from Western Christianity, all these lands were
gathered into the Orthodox fold after the 9th century. In the vast
territories of Russia the church spread by two main means. First,

through the success of monasticism as a self-propelled movement that was able to expand into non-Christian territory and establish bridgeheads of further expansion. Second, by the established strategy of entering into partnership with imperial ambition. This strategy proved successful when the Orthodox Church formed an alliance with the increasingly powerful dynasty based in Moscow and became a focus for the construction of Russian unity and identity. The Byzantine model of 'Caesaro-papism', of emperor working closely with church, proved adaptable to this new context. When the Byzantine Empire fell to the Ottoman Turks in 1453, Russia was able to take over the mantle of Christian empire, with Ivan II styling himself Tsar (Caesar, or Emperor) in 1472, and Russia attaining the status of a Patriarchate in 1589.

Though Moscow might now consider itself the 'third Rome', and though Russian Orthodoxy might now challenge Greek Orthodoxy for supremacy, the Patriarch of Constantinople retained considerable power. The Ottomans not only allowed him to remain in office, but regarded him as the spiritual leader of all Orthodox Christians within the extensive Ottoman Empire (including Greeks, Bulgars, Serbs, Arabs, and Albanians). Ironically, the Patriarch's power was challenged less by the success of the Ottoman Empire than by its collapse in the 19th century and by the subsequent exile of Greeks from Turkey. Though he retains the title of 'Ecumenical Patriarch' (patriarch of the inhabited world) and has an honorary primacy within Orthodoxy, the present-day Patriarch's diminished flock consists largely of Greeks living in Crete, the USA, Western Europe, and Australia.

In the modern period churches in the East struggled to maintain their power in the face of growing secular power just as they did in the West. An assertion of ecclesiastical power by Patriarch Nikon in mid-17th-century Russia led not only to reaction in his own church (on the part of the so-called 'Old Believers' who wished to retain traditional Russian customs), but to greater state control. The modernizing Tsar Peter the Great, who reigned between 1682 and

1725, abolished the office of Patriarch and turned the church into a department of state. A reassertion of conservative interests in the 19th century went together with a revival of the church under the banner of 'Orthodoxy, autocracy, and nationality', and led to massive reaction against both church and the ruling classes in the Bolshevik Revolution of 1917.

Given Karl Marx's hostility to religion as an 'opiate of the people' and an obstacle to progress, and given Communist governments' attempts to establish total control over the lives of their people, it is not surprising that the church under Communism was often treated with ruthless hostility. In Russia, for example, the 46,000 churches of the pre-revolutionary era had been reduced to a few hundred by the late 1930s. But the state was also capable of changing its policy toward the churches when politically expedient, as Stalin did during the Second World War when he realized how useful the churches could be in motivating Russians to do their patriotic duty, and in colonizing areas brought under Soviet control. Given Orthodoxy's history of dependence upon political patronage and its tendency to obey the governing authorities, it found itself equipped with few resources to resist state control. In Bulgaria as in Russia, Orthodoxy lost a great deal of credibility as a result of its collaboration with the Communist authorities, whereas in Romania, East Germany, and Poland, Protestant and Catholic churches demonstrated a greater ability to mobilize opposition to the state, particularly in the 1980s as Communism began to fail.

Since the collapse of Communism, Orthodoxy has been attempting to re-establish power in ex-Communist lands, often by way of active cooperation with the new political regimes. Its tendency to support neo-nationalism was demonstrated most dramatically in Serbia, but is also evident in several other countries, including Russia. In the latter, the church has been lobbying the government to prevent other forms of religion, including Christian denominations, from proselytizing ('sheep stealing'). In the West, Orthodoxy continues to play an important role in supporting the ethnic identities of immigrant peoples, but is also developing a new role as a popular religious option for small numbers of affluent and educated Westerners who appreciate its mix of ritualism and mysticism.

As for the Nestorian and non-Chalcedonian ('Monophysite') churches of the East, they too have suffered as a result of wider political developments, though their fate has been shaped more

Eastern Christian churches

1. Eastern Orthodox churches
Ancient Patriarchates: Constantinople, Alexandria, Antioch, Jerusalem

Other Patriarchates and autocephalous (self-governing) churches: Russia, Serbia, Romania, Bulgaria, Cyprus, Greece, Poland, Albania, Georgia, Czechoslovakia, America

Autonomous churches: Finland, Japan

2. 'Separated' churches
Church of the East (also called the Nestorian Church)

Non-Chalcedonian ('Monophysite') churches: Syrian Church of Antioch, Syrian Church of India, Coptic Church (in Egypt), Armenian Church, Ethiopian Church

3. Uniate churches (Orthodox churches that accept the authority of Rome)

There are Uniate churches parallel to the vast majority of the Orthodox churches listed above, with the largest groups in the Ukraine, Romania, India, Syria, and Lebanon.

by the energies of Islam than of Communism. The upsurge of exclusivistic forms of Islam in much of the contemporary Middle East threatens to eliminate the few remaining churches that still stand as a testament to those ancient forms of Eastern Christianity that refused to accept the 'Orthodox' consensus.

Western missionary activity

By the late Middle Ages, the Western church seemed to have reached the limits of possible expansion, especially when its attempts to push back the boundaries of Islam by way of the Crusades failed. But the late 15th century saw new possibilities opening up as increasingly powerful nation states, particularly Spain and Portugal, began to extend their empires overseas, most notably in the Americas.

The latter development initiated the first phase of Western Christian expansion overseas, a phase that spanned the 16th and 17th centuries and ended in the 18th. A number of features distinguish it from a second phase of Christian mission that followed a century later. First, this was chiefly a phase of Roman Catholic expansion. Although the Protestant churches inherited Christianity's universalizing and expansive drive, their evangelistic energies were initially focused within Europe rather than outside it. Second, it is almost impossible to distinguish political and religious motives, energies, and results in the first phase of Christian mission (Spain and Portugal were both Catholic powers; their monarchs were religious as well as political leaders and the Pope gave them full authority over the churches in the territories they conquered; the conquest of South America was undertaken for gold, slaves, land, and souls and under obedience to king, Pope, and God). Third, this mission involved the wholesale export of Western culture and institutions. To be baptized was to become a Christian and to accept Spanish or Portuguese rule. As in medieval Europe, it was more important to belong to 'Christendom' than to confess the faith on an individual basis. Finally, the faith was spread by conquerors, friars, and clergy. As yet there were no specially commissioned agents of evangelization called 'missionaries'.

Thus the first phase of Christian expansion remained largely medieval in its methods and assumptions, even though it was made possible by early modern developments, including improved transport by sea and the rise of powerful independent nation states. By contrast, the second phase of mission, which lasted throughout the 19th century and into the first part of the 20th, was more characteristically modern. Its approach was shaped by confessional Christianity, both Catholic and Protestant. Instead of creating converts whose Christian allegiance was chiefly evident in outward behaviours such as reception of the church's sacraments and membership of Christian society, modern mission sought a more sincere and informed dedication of heart and mind. In doing so it had new, portable means at its disposal: Bibles, catechisms, confessional statements, and hymn books.

A further difference was that instead of relying upon clergy and members of religious orders, the second phase of mission rationalized the enterprise of evangelization by creating dedicated missionaries. The initial intention was that missionaries should be men drawn from the ranks of the clergy and specially prepared for their role overseas. In reality, however, a shortage of volunteers meant that lay people had to be trained as missionaries, and these were often men who wished to travel abroad with their wives. By the late 19th century, women were playing an increasingly important role in overseas mission, even though they still had to work under the nominal control of a man. Given that women were denied other influential public roles in the churches, the missionary call proved attractive to many (see the next chapter). Catholic women could join one of the new missionary orders, whilst Protestant women could join a missionary team, sometimes composed of just husband and wife. Many female and male missionaries were equipped with practical skills they could employ in the mission field, perhaps in

21. Two missionaries from the Universities' Mission to Central Africa set out on a journey in Tanganyika, c. 1902.

education or medicine – for in the second phase of mission the offer of the gospel often went hand in hand with the offer of some of the 'material benefits' of Western civilization.

The final difference between the first and second phases of mission was that in the latter missionary activity took place in looser alliance with political power. The association between state and church was still important, and modern mission was closely associated with Western colonial expansion. But a distance was often maintained between a Western regime and the missionaries who entered a country under its protection, and there could even be a degree of mutual suspicion and hostility. In some cases, where missionaries from a variety of churches were allowed to operate in the same territory, there could also be intense intra-Christian rivalry. But even when a state refused to throw its weight behind missionary activity, there is no doubt that the latter could benefit by association with colonial power. Missionaries were often the mediators between a colonial power and its subjects, and they provided access to some of the goods of the more powerful society – material, cultural, and spiritual. Though there was also intensive missionary work in areas that did not come under extensive Western colonial control, such as China, it is probably significant that the results were less impressive than when missionary work took place within the context of colonialism. Nevertheless, colonial context was not in itself a guarantee of missionary success.

Christian upsurge in the southern hemisphere

The second phase of Western Christian evangelization had mixed and rather complex results. Biblical Christianity tends to judge success in terms of the number of individual conversions, whilst Church Christianity is more likely to take account of the degree of Christian penetration of society. Taking both criteria into account, the most thoroughgoing mission success must surely be in 'Latin' America, where ruthless religio-political conquest in the first phase of mission followed by more modern forms of missionary activity in the second resulted in widespread Christianization (as also happened in the Philippines). By contrast, the most notable failure has been in lands where Christianity was not backed by colonial power and/or where it was forced to compete with existing religious monopolies, as in China, India, and much of the Middle East. In areas like sub-Saharan Africa, where Christianity found itself in competition with varied forms of indigenous spirituality, there tended to be greater success, though thoroughgoing 'conversion' seems to have been less common than selective appropriation of the cultural and material goods that modern missionaries had to offer.

As well as being aided by alliance with the dominant power of the West, Christian mission could also be hindered by it. Converts could win some significant advantages for themselves and their families by accepting the religion of the colonial power, but they also risked separation from their own culture and people. The more a religion – like Islam or Hinduism – served as a marker of identity, the greater the risk that conversion would be interpreted as an act of cultural betrayal. This was another reason why mission did best where Christianity could be combined with indigenous beliefs and practices, as in Latin America and parts of sub-Saharan Africa. It also helps explain why the most spectacular upsurge of Christianity outside the West occurred after the 1970s, when the withdrawal of Western colonial power eliminated some of the cultural barriers to conversion (the role of rapid population growth must also be taken into account).

This recent Christian upsurge has involved many different sorts of churches: colonial churches (both Protestant and Catholic), independent churches, and new indigenous churches. It is associated, above all, with the pan-denominational movement of Pentecostal or Charismatic Christianity – which may influence or inspire any of the different types of church just mentioned, but which is most closely associated with Biblical Protestantism. The *World Christian Encyclopaedia* estimates that Charismatic Christianity has increased its share from 6.4% of global church members in 1970 to 27.7% in 2000, and that 71% of Charismatics are now non-white, with 66% living in the so-called Third World.

Since the Charismatic upsurge has been more or less contemporaneous with the spread of resurgent Islam, it is interesting to compare the two. Both have flourished in territories that were once under Western colonial control, and both have enjoyed maximum growth in the post-colonial era. Both have a globalizing tendency, and both represent indigenous movements of modernization. To be part of the Islamic or Charismatic upsurge is to be part of a global movement and to lay hold of the resources and sense of universal, triumphant purpose that entails. One's horizons and sense of identity are immediately raised from the local or national to the international, and power is enhanced accordingly. In both instances one also enjoys the benefit of becoming part of a movement of modernization that does not require one to sell one's soul to the Western version of modernity. Through membership one can lay hold of many of the benefits of modernity, including education, technology, and affluence, without having to embrace those aspects of 'secular' Western modernity that are experienced as most alien to one's own culture.

The Charismatic Christian upsurge is differentiated from the Islamic upsurge, however, by at least two factors (both of which make the former appear less threatening to the West than the latter). First, it has much more direct historical and cultural links with the West. Second, it offers more by way of individual than social or political empowerment. Charismatic Christians rarely have much interest in gaining political power, in establishing influence over organized politics, or in changing society by political means. They are generally happy to let secular authorities take care of such matters, whilst they concentrate on the more important business of transforming individual lives.

Such transformation comes about by way of the gift of the Holy Spirit. So central and defining is Charismatic Christianity's emphasis on the Spirit that some scholars refer to the movement as 'third-person Christianity'. As we saw in the last chapter, it has roots in the Pentecostal churches that developed in several parts of the West simultaneously at the start of the 20th century, and quickly spread elsewhere. In the 1970s a wave of 'Charismatic revival' affected churches in both the northern and southern hemispheres,

22. Charismatic worship in Abidjan, Ivory Coast.

and was regarded by its followers as the work of the Spirit gathering in a new harvest of souls. Like Christian Fundamentalists, with whom they have much in common, Charismatics look forward with eager expectation to the end of the world when evil will be destroyed and Christ will return to rule and gather His followers into glory. Unlike Fundamentalists, however, they believe that baptism in the Spirit and reception of charismata (gifts) seals one's salvation. In addition to offering guidance from outside by way of the infallible Word of scripture, God as Holy Spirit enters within. As we noted in the previous chapter, Charismatic Christianity represents a coming together of the Biblical and Mystical varieties of the religion.

As well as engendering eager hope and expectation about future blessedness, Charismatic Christianity offers its followers tangible blessings in the here and now. Those who receive the Holy Spirit are filled with miraculous new powers – to speak in tongues, heal, prophesy, resist evil, and perform God's work. In the process individuals attain a new sense of 'self' and personal significance. They may feel empowered to take more responsibility for their own lives as well as those of others. Some may start their own Christian ministries and set up their own churches. Well-being is also enhanced through the action of fellow Christians, who may offer spiritual, emotional, and material support; and membership of a church often brings benefits of education, health provision, childcare, and welfare.

All these factors help the spread of Christianity in Latin America, sub-Saharan Africa, and parts of Asia. Here, where traditional frameworks of life are left behind as individuals travel to the expanding cities to find work in the global capitalist economy, Christianity helps develop a sense of personal worth independent of traditional social roles, and strengthens individuals' resources for success in the new global capitalist economy. In situations of often desperate poverty and inadequate healthcare, it offers tangible support and material aid and, when all else fails, it offers a miracle.

Liberation Theology

In academic theology the most influential manifestation of the 'indigenization' of Christianity in a post-colonial context was the rise of Liberation Theology in Latin America from the late 1960s. Liberation Theology accused existing theology of being distorted by the privileged (Western, white, male) context in which it was produced. To counteract this bias, it favoured a 'bias to the poor', in which theology would emerge from contexts of struggle and oppression. The method it proposed was to begin with social analysis and social action (making use of Marxist tools) and only then move on to read and interpret the Christian scriptures. This would result in a theology done by the poor for the poor; and because their situation had similarities to that in which Jesus had lived and taught, they would be in a better position to interpret his words than Western academics. Liberation Theology was criticized by Pope John Paul II for being too sympathetic to Marxism, and by others for claiming to be a grassroots movement when in fact it was led 'from above' by academics, priests, and nuns. It inspired 'base communities' of Catholic Christians committed to doing theology together, and to bearing witness to God's Kingdom by way of appropriate forms of political engagement.

The globalization of Christianity

While turn-of-the-millennium Christianity declines in much of the West, it thrives in much of the South. It is estimated that Charismatic Christianity may involve around half a billion people, the vast majority of them located in the southern hemisphere. Some older indigenous and colonial churches are also doing well, not least because of their readiness to adopt elements of the Charismatic spirit. This means that for the first time there are now roughly as many Christians in the southern hemisphere as in the northern (around one billion in each). Since numbers in the South are still growing fast, due to high population growth as well as conversion, whilst those in the North are shrinking, the numerical centre of gravity of Christianity is shifting. Christianity has become a more global religion than ever before, and the long-established dominance of the Western churches can no longer be taken for granted.

A shift in the numerical centre of gravity of Christianity does not, however, inevitably mean a shift in the locus of control. In the case of the Roman Catholic Church, for example, which remains the largest Christian denomination (accounting for around 42% of Christian adherents in 2000), the existing leadership has actively embraced the globalization of the church. More than any previous

Pope, John Paul II (1920-) became a global leader, travelling regularly to every part of the globe and working tirelessly to maintain the unity of the faithful during a period of rapid change. Whilst defending a conservative morality in the sphere of private life and sexual ethics, he built on the liberalizing work of Vatican II in relation to political life, carving out a new role for the papacy and the Roman Catholic Church as a defender of human dignity and human rights. Non-Western bishops and clergy now play a full role in the Catholic Church, and 'enculturation' (the incorporation of elements of indigenous culture into Christian thought and worship) has been actively encouraged. Yet Rome remains the centre of Catholicism, its leadership unchallenged. And the globalization of the Catholic Church takes place not just from grassroots – as in the case of Charismatic Christianity – but under the guidance of clerical authority, an authority that is ultimately accountable to the Pope.

This is not to deny that the South may play an increasingly important role in shaping Christianity, even in determining the policy of the Western churches. Already it is evident that the growing conservatism of the churches in the West that was noted in the previous chapter is starting to be reinforced by antagonism towards Western 'secular liberalism' on the part of many churches in the South. Opposition to homosexual activity within the Anglican and Catholic churches, for example, has been strengthened by opposition on the part of African bishops in both denominations. Like Islam, Christianity may be in the process of becoming a global force of resistance to some of the dominant values of late modern Western culture. As in Islam, the liberal wing of the religion suffers a crisis of confidence in the face of the growing forces of conservatism. In both, post-colonial hostility to Western dominance may ally itself with intra-Western dislike of modern, subjectivized culture – often taking issues of sexual morality as a focus. Unlike Islam, however, Christianity is more likely to launch its challenge by way of personal witness and lobbying than by direct political action.

Conclusion

The geographic profile of Christianity has changed significantly over 2,000 years. In the very broadest terms, one could say that Christianity's centre of gravity in the first millennium lay in the eastern Mediterranean region and that it shifted west and north (to Europe and Russia) in the medieval period. Despite missionary success in parts of the southern hemisphere, first Latin America then parts of sub-Saharan Africa and Asia, the Christian centre of gravity remained in the West and North (Europe, North America, Russia) right through to the 20th century. Only at the very end of that century did the growth of Christianity in the South begin to bring about a shift that established a more truly global profile than ever before. (Nevertheless, there are large parts of the globe where Christianity still has minimal support – even though there is now *some* Christian presence in every nation in the world.)

Taking this chapter together with the last, a pattern seems to have become evident in the last few decades: decline of Christianity in more affluent societies, and growth in poorer parts of the world (it is estimated, for example, that 82% of Charismatics live in poverty, and analysis of the *World Values Surveys* finds that Nigeria, Uganda, the Philippines, and Zimbabwe are amongst the most religious countries in the world). Though it would be too simple to assume a straightforward link between poverty and Christian success, we have noted some lines of connection. Affluent late capitalist societies in the West encourage people to be self-reliant, creative, 'individual', 'enterprising', risk-taking, and concerned with personal well-being (material security makes this possible, and consumption- and service-based economies put a premium on such qualities). The impact on churches that demand conformity to the 'higher' authority of a transcendent God – rather than the cultivation of one's unique life – is negative. In poorer countries, by contrast, there is far less scope for people to turn their backs on social and ethical frameworks of support in order to cultivate their unique lives, and they are more likely to be involved in industries that put a premium on reliability and obedience rather than innovation and creativity. Here religion that demands conformity to higher authority fits much better with the shape of life. Nevertheless, as global capitalism and democratic ideals extend their reach into every part of the world, so the demand for personal empowerment grows – and Christianity succeeds best where it combines the directives of power from on high with the promise of a sacred power that enters directly into subjective-life.

Chapter 7
A woman's religion?

The preceding chapters have made passing reference to the prominent place of women in Christian history. We have noted their presence in the earliest Christian communities, in movements of mystical and monastic piety, in the upheavals of Reformation, in modern missionary work. In the contemporary West women outnumber men by a ratio of three to two in most churches, and though there is little research on this topic, the ratio may be similar in the southern hemisphere.

Our final task in exploring Christian success and failure is to investigate the religion's appeal to the different sexes. The most pressing task is to explain why women appear to be more numerous and more active in the churches whenever and wherever we have hard evidence about such matters. Were we looking at something like goddess spirituality, where women are directly empowered through the invocation of a female divine, the issue would not be so puzzling. But Christianity has traditionally excluded women from positions of power, and often places more emphasis on the connections between divinity and masculinity than divinity and femininity. So in fact we must deal with two questions: not only 'why so many women?', but also 'why not more men'?

The attraction for men

Nowhere in the Bible is it clearly and unambiguously stated that women and men are of equal dignity and worth, that women should never be treated as men's inferiors, that the domination of one sex by the other is a sin, or that the divine takes female form. The closest the New Testament comes to any such statements is in Galatians, where Paul writes, 'There is no longer Jew or Greek, there is no longer slave or free, there is no longer male and female; for you are all one in Christ Jesus'. In I Corinthians, however, Paul explains that women should be veiled in church to signal their subordination to men because 'the head of every man is Christ, and the head of a woman is her husband', and that 'women should keep silence in the churches. For they are not permitted to speak, but should be subordinate, as even the law says.'

Paul's statements exemplify a pattern in Christianity of all varieties. On the one hand, egalitarian statements are backed up in practice by equal access for both sexes to the church's key rituals and sacraments, scriptures, and the promise of salvation. But on the other hand the egalitarian emphasis is contradicted by a symbolic framework that elevates the male over the female, and by organizational arrangements that make masculine domination a reality in church life. Theological statements on the position of women from down the centuries testify not only to the assumption that it is men who have the authority to define women, but to the precautions that have been taken to ensure that women do not claim too much *real* equality with men – in this life at least.

Though the Christian God is sometimes said to be sexless or 'above gender', both the language and the images used to depict Him are overwhelmingly masculine. As we have seen in Chapter 2, He is often depicted by way of the symbols of the highest masculine authority: throne, crown, sceptre, robes, beard. 'He' is Father and Son, King, Judge, Lord, and Master. A hierarchical relation between the sexes is built into the hierarchical scheme that lies at the heart of

Extracts from theological reflection on the position of women

Woman will be saved through bearing children, if she continues in faith and love and holiness, with modesty.

(I Timothy)

The rule remains with the husband, and the wife is compelled to obey him by God's command. He rules the home and the state, wages wars, and defends his possessions . . . The woman, on the other hand, is like a nail driven into the wall. She sits at home . . . She does not go beyond her most personal duties.

(Luther, *Lectures*)

Properly speaking, the business of woman, her task and function, is to actualize the fellowship in which man can only precede her, stimulating, leading, inspiring.

(Karl Barth, *Church Dogmatics*)

The present reflections, now at an end, have sought to recognize, within the 'gift of God', what he, as Creator and Redeemer, entrusts to women, to every woman. In the Spirit of Christ, in fact, women can discover the entire meaning of their femininity and thus be disposed to making a 'sincere gift of self' to others, thereby finding themselves.

(Pope John Paul II, *Mulieris Dignitatem*)

a Christianity of higher power. If the Christian God were truly sexless or above gender, it would be permissible to conceive 'Her' in female as well as in male terms. In actual fact, however, the whole logic of Christianity renders such representation difficult and unusual. Julian of Norwich is famous for speaking of Jesus as 'our mother', and for stressing his nurturing characteristics, but this is part and parcel of her highly unusual theological stance which claims that in God 'there is no wrath at all'. Recent attempts to introduce feminine pronouns and imagery into liturgical worship have been confined to Liberal or Mystical forms of Christianity, and have proved highly controversial.

A masculine bias is also evident in Christian understandings and representations of 'man' (humanity). One of the most influential images in the Christian repertoire is that of God creating human beings, when Adam is created first and Eve is taken from his side (following the account in Genesis 2; see Figs 23 and 24). An obvious implication is that whereas man is made directly in God's image, woman is a secondary and dependent creation – and that the image of God shines more brightly in the former than the latter. This interpretation is reinforced by the observation that Eve succumbed to sin before Adam. Many drew the natural conclusion that if woman is to be saved she must discipline her body and her bodily appetites more harshly than a man, since it is these appetites that brought about the Fall of the human race, and her sex that separates her from the sacred. The importance of virtues like humility, obedience, and chastity tend to be emphasized for Christian women more than Christian men. The ultimate aim may be the destruction of the female body, so that a sexless but 'manly' spirit may float free. In early Christianity women who attained the same spiritual heights as men (through martyrdom, for example), were frequently spoken of as 'female men of God' who had 'became male'. The imagery of 'putting on Christ', 'becoming part of the body of Christ', and becoming 'sons by adoption' reinforced the idea that salvation for women consisted in subduing or destroying their sex in order to replace it with something of higher value. For men, by contrast,

23 and 24. Creation of Adam and Eve by Michelangelo (Sistine Chapel, 1508–12). The dignity of Adam's creation, in which God brings forth a being made in His image, stands in contrast to the creation of Eve, who steps out of Adam's side stooping and cowed, facing a God very different from herself.

salvation consisted in perfecting the divine nature in whose image they are created from the outset.

The idea of a natural connection between masculinity and divinity is reinforced by the institution of male priesthood – and vice versa. As we saw in Chapter 3, Church Christianity located the sacred in material sacraments, but insisted that only men could consecrate, handle, and distribute them. This extraordinary privilege was justified in terms of analogy between God the Father and the priestly 'father', a man's greater ability to represent Jesus Christ, and apostolic succession from a male saviour through an exclusively male line.

The image of God as Father played a particularly important role in shaping Christian life and society. We have noted how, rather than speak of their dominating power, Christian leaders often preferred to represent themselves as exercising paternal care over their 'children': the priestly 'father' over his parish, the 'abbot' (abba = father) over his monastery, the pope (papa = father) over

The female man of God

Even in them that are women in body, the manliness of their souls hides the sex of their flesh.

(Augustine, sermon)

Although she was an insignificant, weak and despised woman, yet she was clothed with the great and invincible athlete Christ.

(2nd-century account of the martydrom of Blandina)

No, you are all women, but I am a man.

(Response of a 17th-century woman Quaker when rebuked by men for preaching)

the church and society. Such language not only excludes women from the exercise of such roles, but appropriates to men the roles of care and compassion in their 'highest' manifestation. When new and potentially lucrative economic roles opened up to women in the late medieval period, the Protestant Reformers made full use of the rhetoric of fatherhood to exclude them not only from ecclesiastical office but from paid employment and civil power, and to confine them to the home. They taught that just as the heavenly Father ruled over His people, so the earthly father had a duty of care and command over wife, children, servants, and other members of the household. If household members disobey they must be punished by fathers for their own good – by force if necessary.

All of which makes it easy to explain the attraction of Christianity to men simply in terms of male self-interest. Christianity benefits men by setting male self-identity on the strongest possible foundation: the image of man is reflected back from God himself. Men also benefit from the way in which the Christian symbolic framework helps the male sex secure a dominant place in society as a whole. It does this not only by legitimating masculine domination, but by de-legitimating female resistance. In addition, Christianity exercises a direct appeal by offering men attractive roles within church life. By limiting these roles to the few – the ordained clergy – Christianity ensured that they would be more prestigious and well rewarded. In recent times the standing of the clergy has fallen in the West, chiefly because there are now so many other lucrative openings available to members of affluent societies. But in previous centuries power and status were reserved for the very few – those whose birth or military prowess enabled them to maintain ownership of scarce resources, chiefly land. In this context church and monastery offered the only routes by which talented men without property could better themselves in social, cultural, and material terms. The rewards for those who reached the top – whether as abbot or bishop – could be immense.

If men really have so much to gain from Christianity, however, why have they not been more active and numerous in the religion? An obvious answer is that Christianity can support masculine domination without requiring that all men be regular or active churchgoers. Indeed, it is more important that women attend church and absorb the Christian message than men do. An additional answer is that the men who are most active in the church are often those who have some office and status there (whether as church warden, altar boy, priest, theologian or bishop). Since Christianity cannot offer rewarding roles to all men, many see no obvious reason to get involved. Sitting passively in the pew and being preached to does not necessarily appeal to those who are used to more active and vocal roles in society, especially when the message being preached has to do with the importance of humility, weakness, submission, and self-sacrificial love.

It is likely, then, that men find some aspects of Christianity difficult, unappealing, or restrictive. Even though the religion confers obvious benefits on the male sex, it exacts a price. Though

Christianity endorses male power, it cautions that it must be exercised in a 'fatherly' way by serving God and others rather than the self (the pope, for example, describes himself as a 'servant of the servants of God'). Similarly, although male sexuality is rendered more visible and less problematic in the Christian scheme of things than female sexuality, it is hardly embraced with wholehearted enthusiasm. It too has to be exercised in a restrained fashion and in fulfilment of God's purposes rather than for pleasure and self-fulfilment. Thus none of the markers of machismo – sexual, material, physical, and political dominance – are given unequivocal support in the Christian tradition, whilst the 'womanly' virtues of love, gentleness, obedience, and self-sacrifice receive more explicit endorsement. This, combined with the fact that there are so many women in the churches, may render Christianity just a little too feminine for some men to tolerate; the costs may be found to outweigh the benefits.

The attraction for women

If Christianity seeks in some ways to 'unman' males, by the same token it has much to offer women. Women benefit in two ways: first, by the restraint that appeal to Christian values may place on the unbridled exercise of male power; and second, by the recognition and affirmation of the value of typically feminine roles, virtues, and dispositions.

Even though the New Testament contains no unambiguous endorsement of female equality, and certainly offers no support to female dominance, there are hints and glimmers of a 'kingdom' in which things could be different. Jesus not only ministers amongst and with women, he teaches that humility, poverty of spirit, and sincere devotion are more important than worldly power or priestly status. He speaks of a love whose exercise knows no limits or distinctions, a love which, as Paul puts it, 'is patient and kind . . . not jealous or boastful . . . not arrogant or rude . . . does not insist on its own way . . . '. Such a message could inspire and empower those whose daily work and care were often ascribed little economic or cultural, let alone spiritual, value.

Christianity could also offer women congenial social space. In theory at least, the church community is bound only by ties of love – love for one another and for the God whose Son gives His life for His church. The resonance with the ethos of the family is striking, and it is no coincidence that the image of the family should be so central to ecclesiastical self-understanding (the church as the 'family of God'). Though this image could be used to reinforce the rule of fathers, it could also have profound significance for those whose daily lives were taken up with the unrewarded tasks of loving, caring, and sacrificing for others. Women with children have much to gain from an institution like the church that supports the family, exalts the domestic role, offers support and companionship in the task of rearing and educating children, and, once children have left home, can find other caring roles for women to perform. In any case, women seem more inclined than men to join a community for the good of community and relationship alone, irrespective of any other roles or privileges that membership might bring.

What is more, for much of Christian history the church has been the only public space that women have been allowed to occupy besides the home – certainly the only one that wives and daughters might be allowed to attend independent of husbands and fathers. The later medieval period saw a flourishing of female piety, still evident in the rich flowering of feminized art and sculpture that occurred at that time, in which images of female saints abound. Despite Protestantism's hostility to such images, some post-Reformation churches offered women new opportunities for education, literacy, and even public ministry. In the 19th century, missionary work and charitable activities offered women an outlet for energies and ambitions that would otherwise have been frustrated. Though the avowed aim of (for example) female-led temperance movements might be to curb the consumption of alcohol, the deeper concern was often to bridle men and machismo – male spending, male sexuality, and male violence. Even though it could not be made explicit, such organizations sometimes harboured elements of a feminist agenda. Churchmen might have become worried about such activities, but it was hard to control women who claimed to be carrying out the injunctions of Christ. Though the scriptures had more often been used to justify male control of women, it was possible for the tables to be turned.

But even if Christianity can attract women by affirming feminine virtue and providing congenial social space and tools of resistance to masculine domination, does not its close association of masculinity and divinity have the opposite effect? Not necessarily. In fact, women may be more attracted to the worship of a male God and saviour than men, and the reason is not hard to see. If society encourages women to love, serve, obey, and even worship men, then it is not difficult to transfer such attitudes to a male God – or for devotion to a male God to reinforce such behaviours. Indeed, in so far as society reinforces heterosexuality, it is much more natural for a woman to offer intense, emotional devotion to a male deity than for a man to do the same. Whilst men may have no difficulty in bowing down before the power, majesty, and fatherly authority of God, they are less likely than women to 'give their hearts to Jesus' or enter into an intense, emotional relationship with him. We noted the development of romantic, erotic forms of mystical piety in earlier chapters. 'Brides of Christ' would surrender to Christ the heavenly bridegroom and feel themselves melting into him. Such imagery is not confined to the past. In many Biblical and Charismatic Christian circles today women still engage in romance with Christ, and still affirm – to quote one Evangelical 'bride' – that 'Jesus alone understands me, forgives me and loves me'.

Such erotic piety may have different social and personal implications. It may reinforce patriarchal norms and encourage women to accept forms of male domination to which they would not otherwise be willing to submit. It may offer women a means of coping with such domination, but prevent them from questioning

25. *Vision of the Sacred Heart of Jesus* by Antonio Ciseri (Church of Sacro Cuore, Florence, 1880). Mary Margaret Alacoque (1647–90), depicted here, was the first to receive a vision of the Sacred Heart of Jesus. By the 19th century, statues and pictures of the Sacred Heart could be found in many Roman Catholic churches, homes, and schools. They have been particularly important in female devotion.

the social order of which it is a part. Or it may equip them with an effective means of resisting male domination and constructing different social arrangements. In Catholicism, for example, 'brides of Christ' could – and still can – escape earthly marriage altogether by entering a convent where they gather with like-minded women and may attain considerable independence from men.

In the context of patriarchal societies, Christianity may therefore appeal to women *because* of its masculine bias, rather than in spite of it. Christianity may have much to offer women who wish to turn their backs on power and embrace the virtues of love, humility, powerlessness, and self-sacrifice. But it also has a considerable amount to offer those who want some share in such power. For if power is concentrated in a male God and His church, there is much more to be gained by joining it than by rejecting it. Not only could Christian women claim the protection of the Almighty Father God, they could also enter into a relationship with Him that was every bit as close and intense as that enjoyed by a man. By such means a handful of women in Christian history have claimed the right to do theology, to speak for themselves, even to command kings and popes; in the societies in which they lived it is hard to imagine any other route by which they could have done so.

The contemporary situation

Christianity can no longer take male domination for granted, for the societies in which it is situated have been changing – particularly in the West. Of the several unprecedented changes that took place in advanced industrial societies in the last quarter of the 20th century, the move towards gender equality has been one of the most significant. Whilst genuine equality remains an elusive ideal, as an ideal at least it is now widely accepted. A recent survey of cultural values worldwide indicates that such acceptance is now the single most important cultural item separating affluent Western societies from less economically developed countries in the rest of the world. The difference can be traced back not only to cultural and educational differences, but to the much greater scarcity of resources outside the West. Where money and jobs are in short supply, men have always been more likely to try to preserve a monopoly than when they have nothing to lose by allowing women (relatively) free access to the labour market.

Of the many threats that Christianity has to face in modern times, gender equality is one of the most serious, though perhaps the most underestimated by the churches. The more radical feminists had Christianity in their sights from the start. When Elizabeth Cady Stanton (1815–1902) set out to liberate women from their traditional shackles, for example, one of her first projects was a *Woman's Bible* in which the passages used by men to keep women in subjection were highlighted and critiqued. Although some early campaigners for female emancipation belonged to the churches, and though some church-related movements helped nurture women's entrance onto the public stage, the campaigners who embraced the feminist cause most wholeheartedly nearly always made a break from Church and Biblical Christianity (Mystical Christianity sometimes proved more compatible with feminism).

The rift between Christianity and feminism was exacerbated not so much by the churches' opposition to the cause, but by their general indifference. Even churches that supported the emancipation of slaves, the amelioration of the condition of the industrial working class, and the civil rights movement of the 1960s often failed to give similar support to the cause of women's liberation. So far as their own institutional life was concerned, a few of the more liberal Biblical and Mystical churches supported women's ministry as early as the late 19th century, but Church Christianity and conservative Biblical Christianity opposed the ordination of women with vigour. The Roman Catholic and Orthodox churches still refuse even to discuss the possibility of women's ordination.

An obvious consequence of the churches' continuing failure to support gender equality – in practice if not in theory – is the

Feminist Theology

Feminist Theology developed in the 1970s, hand in hand with Second Wave Feminism. It represents an attempt to write theology on the basis of women's experience, and in so doing to reform the Christian tradition from within.

The earliest major voice in Feminist Theology also turned out to be one of the most critical. When she wrote *The Church and the Second Sex* in 1968, Mary Daly believed that the church and theology could be reclaimed and reformed by feminists. By the time she published *Beyond God the Father* in 1973, she had come to the conclusion that Christianity was irredeemably patriarchal. In her later works she developed a 'Post-Christian' position which encouraged women to abandon the 'phallocentric' world of Christianity and develop their own authentic forms of spirituality in isolation from men. As she says in *Pure Lust* (1984): 'We do not wish to be redeemed by a god, to be adopted as sons, or to have the spirit of a god's son artificially injected into our hearts, crying "father".'

A second major contributor to Feminist Theology, Rosemary Radford Ruether, has also written about the importance of women retreating into 'womanchurch' and creating their own rituals, prayers, and theologies. But Ruether has never abandoned her ultimate aim, which is to reform Christianity by calling it back to what she views as the prophetic, egalitarian mission and message of Jesus. In *Sexism and God-Talk* (1983) she argues that:

> The uniqueness of feminist theology lies not in its use of the criterion of experience but rather in its use of women's experience, which has been almost entirely shut out of theological reflection in the past. The use of women's experience in feminist theology, therefore, explodes as a critical force, exposing classical theology ... as based on male experience rather than on universal human experience.

> Here and in later works Ruether argues that the integration of women's experience into Christianity will result in a rather different religion in which 'God/ess' will be more feminized and more immanent, in which self-affirmation and development will be emphasized as much as sinfulness, and in which egocentric dreams of post-mortem existence will be abandoned in favour of a celebration of life in its wholeness here and now.

alienation of women and men sympathetic to the ideal. This is not to say that huge numbers of women leave the churches in a conscious act of protest, but that one of the reasons that each successive generation since the 1960s has been less likely to attend than the one before may be that many women and men are no longer in sympathy with the churches' implicit or explicit messages about gender roles. Women who refuse to submit to male authority may struggle with a religion that has male clergy, a male God, and a male saviour; and women who want a career on equal terms with men may be alienated by churches that privilege women's domestic roles. They may abandon Christianity altogether, try to reform it, or find themselves attracted to the new holistic forms of spirituality that tend to be run by women for women and which offer direct benefit in terms of personal empowerment.

But this cannot be the whole story, for despite women's defection from the churches (the single most important direct cause of congregational decline), they continue to attend in larger numbers than men. For some, it would seem, the traditional attractions of Christianity remain, not least its ability to affirm women's domestic roles and offer support to family life. Large numbers of women continue to enjoy the satisfactions of an intense relationship with Jesus Christ. Others, particularly in some of the more liberal and mystical forms of Christianity, are experimenting with new forms of spirituality that require less by way of female submission. Some women have been admitted to positions of authority in the church, and a handful have even become bishops.

In the southern hemisphere the story is different again, for here the number of women in the churches is growing rather than declining, and women play a significant rule in Christianity's recent growth. Although a traditional message about male headship is more common than in the West, masculine authority is tempered in Charismatic Christianity by the presence of the Holy Spirit. Not only can the Spirit be represented in feminine terms as gentle, flowing, loving, and nurturing, it also offers direct empowerment to all who admit it into their lives, irrespective of their sex. Far from remaining external, commanding, and forbidding, God as Spirit enters into the most intimate relationship with the believer, empowering from within. Rather than imposing its will from above, the Spirit works through individual lives, bodies, and personalities, conferring authority as it does so. Lest the empowered overreach themselves, however, the Spirit is checked by the Word. That which is contrary to scripture – and thus to male headship – may be condemned as the work of evil spirits rather than the Spirit of God. Given lack of support for gender equality in many of the poorer countries of the world, this message supports a wider social consensus.

Conclusion

The success of Christianity across the centuries may lie, in part, in the delicate balance it has managed to maintain between male and female interests. While supporting the former, it has also made significant concessions to the latter. While affirming masculine domination, it has tempered and qualified it by emphasizing the importance of the gentler, more loving, more feminine virtues. While presenting a rhetoric of egalitarianism, it has ensured that male privilege has been firmly embedded in its own life. In this way it has been able to uphold patriarchal arrangements, whilst subjecting them to critique and control. Equally, it has managed to affirm women and appeal to them, without encouraging them to rebel against their masters. By appealing to greater numbers of women than to men, but in retaining and supporting male control, it may have achieved the best possible outcome in the male-dominated societies of which it has been an integral part.

The shift towards gender equality in modern Western societies poses a serious threat to traditional Christian imagery, teaching, and organization. For men, Christianity's role in reinforcing masculine domination becomes less relevant, whilst for women its usefulness as a way of gaining access to male power and subverting it from within becomes less important. As women as well as men come to place greater authority on the value of their own unique subjective-lives, they become more resistant to the ready-made roles into which the church would have them fit – however highly exalted. Outside the West, however, where full gender equality wins far less support, Christianity's delicate balancing act continues to prove effective. One might say that Christianity is most successful as a 'woman's religion' when it finds itself in a 'man's world' – a world it helps to reinforce, whilst ameliorating its excesses

Conclusion

This book has attempted to profile some of the main types and characteristics of Christianity, and to indicate how they have contributed to its growth and decline at different times and in different places.

The main thrust of its argument has been that Christianity developed an early preference for power from on high, particularly the power of 'fathers', which was strengthened through alliance with political regimes and social orders that shared this preference. This orientation served the religion well, not only by fostering strong and unifying forms of internal organization, but by helping secure the support of secular power. Not that this preference was simply pragmatic: it was based on attraction to the unique figure of the God-man, Jesus Christ, interpreted as the only Son of a loving Father God who dwells in the heavens and creates and controls all things. By acknowledging the power of this God, and offering Him praise and reverence, the believer could be assured of His protection and fatherly care, and be inspired by His Spirit of love.

Thus the dominant trend in Christianity became one that submits itself to higher power, and which strives to bring life into conformity with a transcendent standard that both inspires and judges. For Church Christianity such power is chiefly displayed in the sacramental life of the church; for Biblical Christianity in the teachings of holy scripture. This orientation tends to denigrate the human, with its 'sinful' impulses and desires, and to exalt the divine. Salvation consists in allowing the latter to overrule the former. By contrast, Mystical Christianity identifies sacred power not only with power from above, but with a power that comes from within. Here God is not just Father and Son but Holy Spirit – the animating principle of life. As such, the divine enters directly into the hearts of men and women, diminishing or even closing the distance between the human and the godly in the process. We have also noted, however, that in practice the three 'ideal types' can overlap, most notably when Church or Biblical Christianity incorporate elements of Mystical Christianity.

Whereas the appeal of Church and Biblical Christianity lies in their ability to provide the believer with an objective, external source of meaning, protection, and power, the appeal of a fully inward form of Mystical Christianity lies in its ability to enhance, empower, and validate one's own unique subjective-life. In practice, however, a mysticism which closes the gap between the divine and the human – and brings power wholly within – has been rare and marginal within Christianity. Although we have noted instances when the mystical tendency has floated free in Christianity, we have seen that it is more common for it to shelter within the embrace of Church Christianity or Biblical Christianity. With regard to the former, we noted the rise of a sacramental mysticism in which the individual must destroy their own inner life in order to make way for Christ (taken within by way of the Eucharistic sacrament); and with regard to the latter, we have traced the rise of Charismatic and Charismatic-Evangelical forms of Christianity in which God's (external) Word remains authoritative, but is supplemented by the (inner) gift of the Holy Spirit.

The latter combination of Biblical and Mystical Christianity has been the most successful of all forms of Christianity in the late 20th century, and the success of Charismatic Christianity worldwide has just about compensated for serious decline in other varieties of

Christianity. The greatest decline has been experienced by Church Christianity in the West, particularly since the 1960s. The liberalization of the latter helped it survive the challenges of 'first modernity' and make a major contribution to Western society and culture, but proved insufficient to help it cope with the threat posed by 'second modernity'. Whereas Liberal Church Christianity was able to lend its support to first modernity's celebration of human reason and human dignity (both external, objective values that can be 'preached'), it has found second modernity's emphasis on the importance of individuals (men *and* women) pursuing their own unique life-paths on the basis of their own deepest convictions, experiences, and intuitions far less agreeable. By contrast, Biblical Christianity has managed to accommodate the turn to subjective-life by emphasizing the experiential satisfactions of being 'born again' in the Holy Spirit. But even such Charismatic subjectivism has failed to appeal widely in the West, where its insistence upon the external authority of the Word of God has proved uncongenial to those who prefer to seek the sacred in their own ways and on their own terms. The latter may turn to new forms of 'holistic' spirituality which promise to enhance subjective-life, or may abandon the sacred altogether.

Elsewhere in the world, we see a rather different picture. In Latin America, sub-Saharan Africa, parts of Asia, and some former Communist lands, Christianity has experienced significant growth in recent decades, with Charismatic forms of Christianity generally faring best. The combination of Biblical and Mystical themes seems to offer 'the best of both worlds' to individuals and societies who are able to gaze on the affluence of the West and work within the global capitalist economy, but who are unable to participate fully in their rewards. On the one hand, such Christianity continues to offer power and authority from on high: the power of a God who will protect and save in this life and the next, the authority of a Biblical teaching that provides clear meaning, support, and guidance. On the other hand, it does not simply call for submission to external authority, but offers individual empowerment from within by way of the gift of the Holy Spirit.

Looking to the future, we are likely to see a continuing decline in support for Christianity in the West, so long as a majority continue to embrace the turn to subjective-life. For those who do not, particularly those who value 'traditional' forms of community and family life, Christianity may continue to serve as a cultural alternative. In less affluent parts of the world, by contrast, Christianity is likely to enjoy continuing success – unless such countries begin to develop their own versions of a turn to subjective-life. In the meantime, Christianity does best where it is able to combine its longstanding support for higher power with the offer of sacred power flowing in and through one's own life and experience.

Source material

Statisfied information cited in this book is derived from:

1. My own research in Kendal, Cumbria, with Paul Heelas and others. See Paul Heelas and Linda Woodhead, *The Spiritual Revolution: Why Religion is Giving way to Spirituality* (Oxford 2003).
2. David Barrett, George Kurian, and Todd Johnson, *World Christian Encyclopedia*, 2nd edn (New York, 2001).
3. The statistical surveys and publications of Peter Brierley. See, for example: Peter Brierley *The Tide is Running Out: What the English Church Attendance Survey Reveals* (London: Christian Research, 2000); Peter Brierley (ed.) *UK Christian Handbook: Religious Trends 3 (2002-2003)* (London: Christian Research, 2001).
4. Research in the USA by Mark Chaves, and, Kirk Hadaway, Penny Marler. See, for example: Kirk Hadaway, Penny Marler, and Mark Chaves, 'What the polls don't show: a closer look at US church attendance', *American Sociological Review* (1993) 58: 741–52; Penny Marler and Kirk Hadaway, 'Attendance', in *Contemporary American Religion*, vol. 1, Wade Clark Roof (ed.) (New York, 2000), pp. 40–2.
5. Ronald Inglehart and Pippa Norris, *Rising Tide: Gender Equality and Cultural Change Around the World* (Cambridge, 2003).

Further reading

General

For a fuller treatment of themes touched on in this book, see:

Linda Woodhead, *An Introduction to Christianity* (Cambridge, 2004)

Paul Heelas and Linda Woodhead, *The Spiritual Revolution: Why Religion is Giving Way to Spirituality* (Oxford, 2005)

Chapter 1
The historical Jesus

E. P. Sanders, *The Historical Figure of Jesus* (London, 1993)

Dominic Crossan, *Jesus: A Revolutionary Biography* (San Francisco, 1995)

New Testament images of Jesus

Paula Friedrikson, *From Jesus to Christ: The Origins of the New Testament Images of Jesus* (Yale, 1988)

Earliest Christianity

Walter Bauer, *Orthodoxy and Heresy in Earliest Christianity* (Philadelphia, 1971)

Chapter 2
Augustine

Peter Brown, *Augustine of Hippo: A Biography* (London, 1967)

Jesus in art and history

Gabriele Finaldi (ed.), *The Image of Christ* (Yale, 2000)

Jaroslav Pelikan, *Jesus Through the Centuries: His Place in the History of Culture* (Yale, 1999)

The culture of Christianity

Geoffrey Barraclough (ed.), *The Christian World: A Social and Cultural History* (London, 2003)

Christian worship

James F. White, *A Brief History of Christian Worship* (Abingdon, 1993)

Chapter 3
Christianity and empire

Ramsey MacMullen, *Christianizing the Roman Empire* (Yale, 1984)

The rise of Christendom

Judith Herrin, *The Formation of Christendom* (Princeton, 1989)

Peter Brown, *The Rise of Western Christendom: Triumph and Diversity AD 200–1000* (Malden, 1996)

Medieval Christianity

R. W. Southern, *Western Society and the Church in the Middle Ages* (Penguin History of the Church) (Harmondsworth, 1990)

Jacques Le Goff, *Medieval Civilization 400–1500* (Oxford, 1988)

Medieval theology

Jaroslav Pelikan, *The Growth of Medieval Theology (600–1300)* (Chicago, 1978)

Protestant Reformation

Patrick Collinson, *The Reformation* (London, 2003)

Diarmaid MacCulloch, *Reformation: Europe's House Divided 1490–1700* (London, 2003)

Catholic Reformation

Michael Mullett, *The Catholic Reformation* (London, 1999)

Early asceticism and monasticism

Peter Brown, *The Body and Society: Men, Women and Sexual Renunciation in Early Christianity* (London, 1990)

Western monasticism

C. H. Lawrence, *Medieval Monasticism: Forms of Religious Life in Western Europe in the Middle Ages* (London, 2000)

Mysticism: East and West

Bernard McGinn and John Meyendorff (eds) *Christian Spirituality*, two volumes (London, 1985; 1987)

Protestant radicalism

George H. Williams, *The Radical Reformation* (Philadelphia, 1962)

Chapter 5
Confessional Christianity

Felipe Fernández-Armesto and Derek Wilson, *Reformation: Christianity and the World, 1500–2000* (London, 1996)

Christianity and the French Revolution

John McManners, *The French Revolution and the Church* (London, 1969)

Christianity in America

Sydney E. Ahlstrom, *A Religious History of the American People* (Yale, 1972)

Fundamentalism and evangelicalism

George Marsden, *Understanding Fundamentalism and Evangelicalism* (Grand Rapids, 1991)

Christianity in the modern West

Hugh McLeod, *Religion and the People of Western Europe 1789–1990* (Oxford, 1997)

Modern theology

David Ford (ed.), *The Modern Theologians* (Oxford, 1997)

Chapter 6
The global history of Christianity

Adrian Hastings (ed.), *A World History of Christianity* (London, 2000)

The Orthodox Church

J. M. Hussey, *The Orthodox Church in the Byzantine Empire* (Oxford, 1990)

Stephen Runciman, *The Orthodox Churches and the Secular State* (London, 1971)

Jane Ellis, *The Russian Orthodox Church: A Contemporary History* (London, 1986)

Orthodox theology

Jaroslav Pelikan, *The Spirit of Eastern Christendom* (600–1700) (Chicago, 1974)

Mission

Andrew Walls, *The Missionary Movement in Christian History: Studies in the Transmission of Faith* (Edinburgh, 1996)

Charismatic upsurge

David Martin, *Pentecostalism: The World their Parish* (Oxford, 2001)

Chapter 7
Women in Christian thought

Elizabeth A. Clark, *Women and Religion: The Original Sourcebook of Women in Christian Thought* (San Francisco, 1997)

Women in medieval Christianity

Eileen Power, *Medieval Women* (Cambridge, 1975)

Caroline Walker Bynum, *Jesus as Mother: Studies in the Spirituality of the High Middle Ages* (Berkeley, 1982)

Women in post-Reformation Christianity

Merry E. Wiesner-Hanks, *Christianity and Sexuality in the Early Modern World* (London, 2000)

Men and Christianity

Andrew Bradstock *et al.*, *Masculinity and Spirituality in Victorian Culture* (MacMillan, 2000)

Richard A. Schoenherr and David Yamane, *Goodbye Father: The Celibate Male Priesthood and the Future of the Catholic Church* (Oxford, 2002)

Chronology

Martin Luther	1483–1546 CE
John Calvin	1509–64 CE
Luther excommunicated; Protestant Christianity begins to take shape	1521 CE
Henry VIII takes control of the new 'Church of England'	1534 CE
Council of Trent	1545–63 CE
Russia becomes a Patriarchate	1589 CE
Foundation of the first Baptist Church in England	1612 CE
Pilgrim Fathers set sail for America	1620 CE
George Fox organizes the Society of Friends	1647 CE
Conversion of John Wesley, founder of Methodism	1740 CE
Friedrich Schleiermacher	1768–1834 CE
Unitarianism organized in America	1815 CE
Karl Barth	1886–1968 CE
Second Vatican Council	1962–5 CE
John Paul II elected Pope	1978 CE
Election of first woman bishop in Church Christianity (Barbara Harrison, Episcopal Church)	1988 CE
Total number of Christian adherents reaches two billion worldwide, with equal numbers in North and South	2000 CE

Index

Expand your collection of
VERY SHORT INTRODUCTIONS

Visit the
VERY SHORT
INTRODUCTIONS
Web site

www.oup.co.uk/vsi

➤ **Information** about all published titles

➤ News of **forthcoming books**

➤ **Extracts** from the books, including titles not yet published

➤ **Reviews** and views

➤ **Links** to other **web sites** and main OUP web page

➤ Information about **VSIs in translation**

➤ **Contact** the editors

➤ **Order** other **VSIs** on-line

THEOLOGY
A Very Short Introduction
David F. Ford

This Very Short Introduction provides both believers
and non-believers with a balanced survey of the central
questions of contemporary theology. David Ford's inter-
rogative approach draws the reader into considering the
principles underlying religious belief, including the central-
ity of salvation to most major religions, the concept of
God in ancient, modern, and post-modern contexts, the
challenge posed to theology by prayer and worship, and
the issue of sin and evil. He also probes the nature of
experience, knowledge, and wisdom in theology, and
discusses what is involved in interpreting theological
texts today.

> 'David Ford tempts his readers into the huge resources of
> theology with an attractive mix of simple questions and
> profound reflection. With its vivid untechnical language it
> succeeds brilliantly in its task of introduction.'
> **Stephen Sykes, University of Durham**

> 'a fine book, imaginatively conceived and gracefully writ-
> ten. It carries the reader along with it, enlarging horizons
> while acknowledging problems and providing practical
> guidance along the way.'
> **Maurice Wiles, University of Oxford**

www.oup.co.uk/vsi/theology

THE BIBLE
A Very Short Introduction
John Riches

It is sometimes said that the Bible is one of the most
unread books in the world, yet it has been a major force
in the development of Western culture and continues to
exert an enormous influence over many people's lives.
This Very Short Introduction looks at the importance
accorded to the Bible by different communities and
cultures and attempts to explain why it has generated
such a rich variety of uses and interpretations. It explores
how the Bible was written, the development of the
canon, the role of Biblical criticism, the appropriation
of the Bible in high and popular culture, and its use for
political ends.

'John Riches' clear and lively Very Short Introduction
offers a distinctive approach to the Bible ... a distin-
guished addition to the series.'

Christopher Rowland, University of Oxford

'Short in length, but not in substance, nor in interest. A
fascinating introduction both to the way in which the
Bible came to be what it is, and to what it means and
has meant for believers.'

Joel Marcus, Boston University

www.oup.co.uk/vsi/bible

PAUL
A Very Short Introduction
E. P. Sanders

Paul is the most powerful human personality in the history of the Church. A missionary, theologian, and religious genius, he laid down in his epistles the foundations on which later Christian theology was built. In this highly original introduction to Paul's life and thought, E. P. Sanders, whose research on Paul has substantially influenced recent scholarship, pays equal attention to Paul's fundamental convictions and the sometimes convoluted ways in which they were worked out.

'Sanders' book is designed to be rounded and comprehensive and fulfils that specification magisterially and with as little technicality as one can sensibly ask.'

J. L. Houlden, *Times Literary Supplement*

'He presents Paul, for all his inconsistencies, with great clarity and insight. . .The book is an apt introduction to Paul; a bold confrontation of the boldest of Christian theologians. . .his interpretation is eloquent for his generation and historically a clear advance.'

Church Times

www.oup.co.uk/isbn/0-19-285451-8